MID DAY MEAL SCHEME AND SCHOOL EDUCATION

About the Author

Dr. P.C. Sikligar presently associated with National Institute of Rural Development, North-Eastern Regional Centre (NIRD-NERC) Guwahati has been concentrating on social security for poor rural masses. He is sole author of five books covering Social Security, Atrocity on Scheduled Castes and Scheduled Tribes, Empowerment of Tribal Women—Wavli, Tribal Development, Deforestation and Tribal Social Life. He has also co-authored four books published by NIRD, Hyderabad with contribution of 55 articles in various national and international journals.

Mid Day Meal Scheme
and
School Education

Planning Implementation and Effectiveness

P.C. Sikligar

CONCEPT PUBLISHING COMPANY PVT. LTD.
NEW DELHI-110 059

ISBN-13: 978-81-8069-787-6

First Published 2011

Published and Printed by

Concept
Since 1974

Concept Publishing Company Pvt. Ltd.

Regd. Office :

A/15-16, Commercial Block, Mohan Garden,
New Delhi-110059 (India)

Phones : 25351460, 25351794, *Fax* : 091-11-25357109

Email : publishing@conceptpub.com

Website : www.conceptpub.com

Editorial Office :

H-13, Bali Nagar, New Delhi-110 015. India.

Cataloging in Publication Data--*Courtesy:* D.K. Agencies (P) Ltd. <docinfo@dkagencies.com>

Sikligar, P. C. (Poonamchand), 1954-

Mid Day Meal Scheme and school education : planning implementation and effectiveness/ P.C. Sikligar.

p. cm.

Includes bibliographical references (p.) and index.

ISBN 9788180697876

1. Mid Day Meal Scheme (India). 2. School children--Food--India--Evaluation. 3. School children--Food--Government policy--India. 4. Education, Primary--India. I. Title.

DDC 371.7160954 22

Dedicated to
My Parents
Shri Nathuji &
Smt. Suraj Bai

Preface

Education is the root of modernization and human development. Education is a process of learning and it continues throughout the life. Education promotes mobilization and encourages people to participate in development activities. Education makes people skilled towards jobs and creates productive efficiency. To promote education, Government of India grants financial assistance and loan to the States and Union Territories on different issues like (1) opening and maintenance of ashram schools, (2) provide hostel facilities, (3) organizing and developing teaching materials, (4) awarding stipends for primary and high school's students, (5) supplying reading and writing materials, (6) giving dress and uniform to the students, (7) exempting Scheduled Caste and Scheduled Tribe candidates from tuition fees, (8) provides pre- and post-matric scholarship from class I to higher education/ professional courses, (9) made arrangement of mid day meals to the students. The National Programme on Nutritional Support to Primary Education popularly known mid day meals scheme is one of the ambitious schemes, which has been implementing since August 1995 throughout the country. This programme intended to give a boost to universalization of primary education by increasing enrolment, retention and attendance and simultaneously impacting upon nutritional status in primary classes. It involved provision of lunch free of cost to school children in all working days. This scheme gives great relief to the parents who are economically not sound and who encourage child labour to meet necessity of the family.

This book is outcome of the study on "Strategies Adopted in Implementation of Mid Day Meal Scheme: A Comparative Analysis". In 2006-07, this study has covered Tamil Nadu,

Gujarat, and Himachal Pradesh, whereas in 2007-08, this study has covered Andhra Pradesh, Uttar Pradesh and West Bengal.

This study concentrates on various aspects, i.e. administrative structure of the committees which constituted from State to Gram Panchayat level, role of the committees, role of the officials engaged at various levels, function the scheme, monitoring, enrolment status of the students, drop-out rate, result of the students, infrastructural facilities available in the schools, student–teacher ratio, problems especially in smooth functions of the scheme, etc.

To carry out this study I got guidance, encouragement and support at various levels. I am grateful to Shri Mathew C. Kunnumkal, IAS, Director General, National Institute of Rural Development (NIRD), Hyderabad, who has always been promoting my academic enthusiasm. I am equally indebted to Shri Banwar Lal, IAS, Deputy Director General (former), National Institute of Rural Development, NIRD, Hyderabad for assigning me the same study on second consecutive year with wide spectrum. I am grateful of Dr. S.K. Bhanj, Professor and Head (Retd.) and Dr. S. Rajakutty, Professor and Head, Centre for Planning, Monitoring and Evaluation (CPME), National Institute of Rural Development (NIRD) for valuable guidance and support to carry out this study timely. I also thank Dr. B. Chakravarty, Professor and Head, Media and Rural Documentation (NIRD), Hyderabad for extensive discussion on various components of the study along with moral support.

I am grateful of Smt. Indra Mallo Jain, IAS, Director, NIRD–North-Eastern Regional Centre (NIRD-NERC), Guwahati for academic support to accumulate this study in book form. I sincerely thank to officials of nodal departments such as revenue, education, social welfare, and rural development department which are involved in implementation of the scheme as well as officials of Food Corporation of India, teachers, members of different committees especially grassroots level, members of the self-help groups, organizers, helpers and cooks, students, etc. who spared their valuable time during fieldwork.

P.C. Sikligar

Contents

Preface	7
List of Tables	10
1. Introduction	15
2. Administrative Structure	45
3. Infrastructure in Schools	95
4. Coverage of the Scheme	105
5. Impact of the Scheme	109
6. Findings and Recommendations	127
Annexure	151
Mid Day Meal Scheme : Central Assistance Admissible to (States/UTs during 2008-09)	
Appendix	153
The Human Right to Food in India	
Bibliography	165
Index	169

List of Tables

1.1 Population and literacy rate of Scheduled Castes and Scheduled Tribes 33
1.2 Enrolment of students in India 34
1.3: Drop out rates in different levels 35
1.4: Foodgrains Allocated and Lifted under Mid Day Meal Scheme in States (2002-03 to 2006-07) 36
1.5 (a) Number of schools covered year-wise in 2006-07 43
(b) Number of schools covered year-wise in 2007-08 43
2.1 Feeding scale age group-wise in Tamil Nadu 46
2.2 Nutritional assessment of diet for the children 46
2.3 Feeding Scale student-wise in Gujarat 53
2.4 Feeding scale cost per child in Gujarat 54
2.5 Feeding Scale in Tribal and Non-tribal areas in Himachal Pradesh 61
3.1 Availability of link road in sample schools of Tamil Nadu, Gujarat and Himachal Pradesh 95
3.2 Availability of electricity in sample schools of Tamil Nadu, Gujarat and Himachal Pradesh 96
3.3 Availability of safe drinking water in sample schools of Tamil Nadu, Gujarat and Himachal Pradesh 96
3.4 Availability of lavatory in sample schools of Tamil Nadu, Gujarat and Himachal Pradesh 97
3.5 Availability of number of rooms in sample schools of Tamil Nadu, Gujarat and Himachal Pradesh 98
3.6 Availability of kitchen sheds in sample schools of Tamil Nadu, Gujarat and Himachal Pradesh 98
3.7 Availability of link road in sample schools of Andhra Pradesh, Uttar Pradesh and West Bengal 99

3.8 Availability of electricity in sample schools of Andhra Pradesh, Uttar Pradesh and West Bengal 100
3.9 Availability of safe drinking water in sample schools of Andhra Pradesh, Uttar Pradesh and West Bengal 100
3.10 Types of sources available for drinking water in sample schools of Andhra Pradesh, Uttar Pradesh and West Bengal 101
3.11 Availability of lavatory in sample schools of Andhra Pradesh, Uttar Pradesh and West Bengal 102
3.12 Availability of rooms in sample schools of Andhra Pradesh, Uttar Pradesh and West Bengal 103
3.13 Availability of kitchen sheds in sample schools of Andhra Pradesh, Uttar Pradesh and West Bengal 104
4.1 State-wise scenario of the scheme (in December 2006) 106
4.2 State-wise scenario of the scheme (in December 2007) 106
4.3 District-wise scenario of the scheme in different states (December 2006) 107
4.4 District-wise status of the scheme (December 2007) 108
5.1 Enrolment, drop-out and result of the sample schools in block Uthirameruru, district Kanchipuram, Tamil Nadu 110
5.2 Enrolment, drop-out and result of the sample schools in block Thripurar, district Kanchipuram, Tamil Nadu 111
5.3 Enrolment, drop-out and result of the sample schools in taluk Himatnagar, district Himatnagar, Gujarat 112
5.4 Enrolment, drop-out and result of the sample schools in taluk Bhiloda, district Himatnagar, Gujarat 113
5.5 Enrolment, drop-out and result of the sample schools in block Gumarwin-I, district Bilaspur, Himachal Pradesh 114
5.6 Enrolment, drop-out and result of the sample schools in block Gumarwin-II, district Bilaspur, Himachal Pradesh 115
5.7 Enrolment, drop-out and result of the sample schools in Mandal Valigonda, district Nalgonda, Andhra Pradesh 116

5.8 Enrolment, drop-out and result of the sample schools in Mandal Baptla, district Guntur, Andhra Pradesh 117
5.9 Enrolment, drop-out and result of the sample schools in Mandal Irla district Rayalaseema, Andhra Pradesh 118
5.10 Enrolment, drop-out and result of the sample schools in block Behjan, district Lakhimpur Kheri, Uttar Pradesh 119
5.11 Enrolment, drop-out and result of the sample schools in block Soran, district Allahabad, Uttar Pradesh 120
5.12 Enrolment, drop-out and result of the sample schools in block Chirala, district Jhansi, Uttar Pradesh 121
5.13 Enrolment, drop-out and result of the sample schools in block Barrackpur–II, district North 24 Parganas, West Bengal 122
5.14 Enrolment, drop-out and result of the sample schools in block Kanksa, district Burdwan, West Bengal 123
5.15 Enrolment, drop-out and result of the sample schools in block Ratua, district Malda, West Bengal 124

Basic education is a foundation,

One should not compromise on this,

Mid day Meal no doubt promotes enrolment,

One should not compromise on education

Qualitative education is backbone of society,

P.C. Sikligar

1

Introduction

Education is the root of modernization and human development. Education cuts across three dimensions such as economic, cultural and political, which are considered the measuring roots of development process. Education is learning process and goes on throughout the life. Education is helpful to lift people above the crude human life and create modern thought. Education promotes mobilization and encourages people to participate in development activities. Education makes people skilled towards jobs and creates productive efficiency. To promote education, Government of India grants financial assistance and loan to the States and Union Territories on different issues like (1) opening and maintenance of ashram schools, (2) provide hostel facilities, (3) organizing and developing teaching materials, (4) awarding stipends for primary and high school's students, (5) supplying reading and writing materials, (6) giving dress and uniform to the students, (7) exempting Scheduled Caste and Scheduled Tribe candidates from tuition fees, (8) providing pre- and post-matric scholarship from class I to higher education, and (9) making arrangement of mid day meals to the students.

The National Programme on Nutritional Support to Primary Education commonly known Mid-day Meals Scheme is one of the ambitious schemes, which began in 1995 at national level. This programme intended to give a boost to universalization of primary education by increasing enrolment, retention and attendance and simultaneously impacting upon nutritional status in primary classes. Mid Day Meal Scheme popularly name for school meal programme in the country. It involved provision of lunch free of cost to school children in all working days. This scheme gives grate relief to the parents who are economically not sound and who encourage child labour to meet necessity of the family. This programme is being implemented by the local bodies/authorities such as Panchayats, Nagarpalika, Local bodies in association with the parent teacher committee, non-Governmental organization/ women DWCRA group and other organizations. Local bodies have got flexibility to decide the type of food to be provided subject to food being wholesome, and having a calorie value equivalent to 100 grams of wheat/rice per student per day. Local bodies are expected to develop institutional arrangement for providing cooked meals to the students. Prior to supply of cooked food, there was a provision to facilitate each student with 3 kg of rice or wheat every month who were securing 80 per cent of attendance every month. This system was prevalent for all the students who were studying in class 1 to 5. This scheme has got objective to boost universalization of primary education and to impart the nutrition of students in primary classes. This scheme has been revised in 2004 and as per the Supreme Court's directive it envisage promising of cooked, nutritious mid day meals to school going children. Importantly, it mentioned about setting up of an appropriate mechanism for quality checks. Despite these developments, over decades, the problems of malnutrition, anemia is very common among the children in India.

To run this scheme at grassroots level, local bodies/ authorities have got power to set up a committee with alive participation of the people to create an awareness of the programme, to generate community support for the programme, the universalizing of participation of all children in primary education, to improve the family and environment of the school, and to ensure that the school functions in terms of broad objectives.

At district level, District Collector is responsible for collection of foodgrains from the Food Corporation of India's godown and arranges transportation of foodgrains and distributes thereof; to the local bodies/schools based on the entitlement of individual school. At the district level the programme may be overseen by a committee under the Chairmanship of District Collector. The committee should include people representatives like Members of Parliament (MPs), Members of Legislative Assembly (MLAs), President of Zilla Parishad, Chairmen of Nagarpalikas and also officials of concerned departments. This committee should *inter alia* create awareness, facilitate and monitor the implementation of programme and further linkage with other related programmes like the Integrated Child Development Scheme, Primary Education and schools health. Similarly, committees also work at Panchayat Samiti or Block level. There is a provision for construction of kitchen shed for preparing of food for the students. This construction could be carried out under Swarnjayanti Gram Rojgar Yojana (SGRY) with the prior permission of the Gram Sabha.

For running the scheme, the non-governmental organizations are selected keeping in view their credentials and capacity to deliver the programme. The Non-Governmental Organizations (NGOs) work in association with the Local Bodies/Village Education Committees/Parent Teacher Association, Women DWCRA (Development of Women and Children in Rural Areas) group, etc. The NGOs ensure that cooked meal to be provided to the children studying in the primary classes only in Government, local body and aided schools.

Effectiveness of the Scheme

Malnutrition is widely prevalent in India among the school going children. Malnutrition not merely gives rise to morbidity and mortality, and prevents a child from developing into a fully functional adult, it adversely affects Universalisation of Elementary Education (UEE) in the following ways: A malnourished child is less likely to attend school regularly, even if such a child does attend school, she finds it difficult to concentrate on and participate in the teaching-learning activities well enough. She, therefore, tends to drop-out, *inter alia,* inability to cope, even if the child does not actually drop-out, her attainment levels tend to be low.

A programme of providing Mid-day meals in schools can be expected to help in universalisation of elementary education in the following ways: By improving enrolment and regularity of attendance; by reducing drop-outs, and by improving children's level of learning and self-esteem. This scheme helps out in elimination of class room hunger, increase enrolment especially girls, surge in daily attendance particularly girls and children belonging to poor sections, curbing of teacher absenteeism, and helping to fill up the gap of social distance which has been existing in India due to strong tie of caste system.

Report of the Committee on Mid-day Meals (1995)

"Provision of free and compulsory education for all children until they complete the age of 14 years is a constitutional goal. According to the policy frame of the Sixth Five Year Plan, reinforced by the 20-point Programme of the Government of India, Universalisation of Elementary Education is to be achieved by 1990. Various measures have been envisaged and undertaken to achieve this goal both at the Central and State levels. One of the important measures is provision of various incentives like free text-books and stationery, free uniforms, attendance, scholarships and mid-day meals. The Mid-day meals programme for primary school children occupies an important place in the overall strategy inasmuch as it would work to alleviate poverty to an extent and at the same time strengthen the educational programme in the country by increasing enrolment, reducing school drop-outs and improving the health of the children thereby bettering their absorption capacity. As the benefits of mid-day meal programme accrue directly to the targeted group, which is fully identified, this would be a very effective programme for alleviation of rural poverty. Considering the potential for giving freshly cooked balanced diet to primary school children, Government of India have decided to launch financial assistance for implementation of such a scheme by the States/ UTs in a phased manner during the Seventh Five Year Plan. The following are the guidelines to be observed by the State Government, in formulating the scheme for submission to the Government of India for sanction.

(i) The scheme should cover all children in primary classes (upto and inclusive of Class IV or Class V, as the case may be) in Government-aided and local body schools. Children in pre-primary classes wherever such classes are functioning as part and parcel of primary schools, will also be covered, provided they are riot covered in the feeding programme under ICDS.

(ii) The scheme should cover all the primary school children by the end of the Seventh Five Year Plan, i.e. by 1989-90. The coverage will be in a phased manner as enumerated below:

(a) In 1985-86, 20 per cent of the total enrolment, as in July, 1985 will be covered.
(b) In 1986-87, 40 per cent of the total enrolments as in July, 1985 and the additional enrolment during the academic year 1985-86 will be covered.
(c) In 1987-88, 60 per cent of the total enrolment as in July, 1985 and the additional enrolments during the academic year 1985-86 and 1986-87 will be covered.
(d) In 1988-89, 80 per cent of the total enrolment as in July, 1985 and the additional enrolments during the academic year 1985-86, 1986-87 and 1987-88 will be covered.
(e) In 1989-90, 100 per cent of the total enrolment as in July, 1985 and the additional enrolments during the academic years 1985-86, 1986-87, 1987-88, and 1988-89 will be covered.

In attempting the coverage mentioned above, it should be ensured that schools in Blocks/Districts are so chosen that all the children in the selected schools are given the mid-day meals. In other words, it should be ensured that in no school some children get meal and some others do not get it.

(iii) A block on which various developmental activities converge would be a compact area for implementation of this scheme as well as for evaluation later. Selection of blocks in the initial phases should appropriately cover the districts which are considered as educationally backward on the basis of low literacy rate, particularly of female literacy. It would be advantageous to select ICDS blocks to start with for implementation of this scheme as they are located in backward areas and urban slums and feeding of pre-school children is already taking place under this scheme. In the selection of blocks, the facilities available for timely supply of foodgrains should also be taken into account.

(iv) For increasing enrolment and retention and improvement of health and nutritional status of children the States should ensure that the schools covered under the mid-day meals scheme, as soon as possible, are covered by a comprehensive school health programme also.

(v) Mid-day meal shall be provided to the children on all school working days (220 in a year).

(vi) Components of mid-day meals and their cost will be as below:

(a) Cereals (100 gms)	20 P
(b) Pulses (10 gms)	7.5 P
(c) Edible Oils (5 gms)	10 P
(d) Condiments and Fuel	10 P
(e) Management and Administration	20 P
Total	67.5 P or say 68P (Paise)

Whereas some components may be changed to suit any state's particular requirements the total cost of the meal would have to be restricted to Re. 0.68 as stated above.

(vii) The expenditure will be shared between Centre and the States/UTs equally. As such the Central assistance to meet this expenditure will be restricted to 34 paise per child per day.

(viii) In computing the Central share of assistance, the existing coverage with CARE assistance will be excluded. This is to ensure that the same children are not counted both under the scheme run with CARE assistance and the Centrally-sponsored scheme. In the states where a scheme of mid-day meal is in operation with partial or universal coverage the Central share will be available only in a graded manner in accordance with the yearly coverage indicated in (ii) above.

(ix) Cereals and, to the extent possible, pulses, edible oils and condiments should be supplied to the schools through an authorised State agency. The stock levels of these commodities in the schools and their further requirements should be monitored at regular intervals to ensure that the prescribed utilisation takes place and that no school runs short of these commodities. Since most of the primary schools are located in villages including the backward and far-flung areas, the State Governments may have to make use of the Civil Supplies Corporation, Cooperative Agencies, or other departmental agencies to establish a delivery system on a regular and efficient basis. The Food Corporation of India would make delivery of the stocks of wheat and rice to the State Government's agency nominated for the purpose only at its depots at the Central issue prices. The nominated State agency would take the cereals from there and pulses, condiments and edible oils separately procured by it to schools. Information about the estimated requirement of grains under the scheme on the basis of the number of children in the primary schools to be covered has to be given to the Department of Food, Government of India separately at the commencement of each year.

(x) The menu for the Mid-day meal scheme should utilise wheat to the maximum extent and utilisation of rice should be discouraged as far as possible. Supply of rice would be restricted to only predominantly rice eating areas. Even there, a modicum of wheat should form part of the scheme. If some other grains locally used are available, the states can utilise them under this scheme.

(xi) The states/UTs would make arrangements for appointment of cooks, helpers and supervisors for implementing this scheme. As far as possible, the cook should be a woman and both the cook and the helper should be from the same village.

(xii) The scheme should provide for necessary involvement of headmasters/teachers. The states should also make other necessary administrative arrangements at various levels such as block, district and state for supervision, management and monitoring. Re. 0.20 per meal provided for management and administration is to cover expenses on all arrangements as well as for purchase of necessary utensils.

(xiii) The scheme should provide for necessary arrangements for proper storage of food materials, cooking and serving food.

(xiv) The scheme should provide for an effective management information system with inbuilt inspection, monitoring, evaluation, etc.

(xv) The States/UTs should seek maximum public cooperation by involving local people's representatives for ensuring regular availability of the materials, their transport, and storage, preparation and serving of meals to the children. Public cooperation in cash and kind should be encouraged.

(xvi) While considerable staff will be needed for efficient of this scheme, care should be taken that no large parallel machinery is created for this purpose. Efforts should be made device a system under which the existing administrative machinery is fully utilised.

(xvii) Whereas tight supervision is required for efficient implementation of the scheme, there should be fullest delegation of powers at every stage of the system for smooth functioning. It has to be ensured that sanctions are issued expeditiously and delays in payment of wages to cooks and helpers are eliminated. The school will need authorisation for drawing rations from the fair price shops. For this purpose efficient mechanism has to be devised. Sufficient advance money should be available to the school for provision of meals at least for a fortnight. This will ensure that meals are served right from the start after vacations and without any break. It would not be necessary to seek sanctions for local expenses from offices/officers above district level. A decentralised but effective arrangement should be made for local purchases, wherever necessary and such purchases should be to the minimum.

(xviii) At the district level there should be a Committee under the chairmanship of the district collector to oversee the implementation of the scheme comprising the functionaries engaged in the implementation of the scheme. The District Education Officer should be the convenor of this committee. It will be the responsibility of this committee to ensure smooth functioning of this scheme with the cooperation of all concerned, so as to remove any bottlenecks that may impede the functioning.

(xix) At the state level, there should be a committee under the chairmanship of the Chief Secretary to overview and monitor this scheme. While Education Secretary will be the convenor, secretaries/heads of concerned departments like rural/community development, cooperation, social welfare, health, civil supplies and food should be represented on this committee. It may meet once in a month in the first year of operation of this scheme and later once in a quarter.

(xx) At the Central level, there will be a Monitoring Committee under the chairmanship of Education Secretary. Planning Commission, Ministry of Finance, Ministry of Social Welfare, Ministry of Health and Family Welfare, Department of Food, Department of Civil Supplies and Food Corporation of India will be represented on this committee. The committee will meet periodically and review/follow-up the implementation of this scheme. The Education Secretary will also from time to time review in meetings with the State Education Secretaries to ensure the smooth functioning of the scheme in the field and get a feedback about the implementation of the scheme.

(xxi) Each State will prepare a scheme in detail for 1985-86 indicating the coverage proposed during 1985-86 and that envisaged in subsequent years of the Seventh Five Year Plan. The scheme should mention infrastructural facilities available, proposals for strengthening the same, financial arrangements, arrangements envisaged for recruitment of staff, preparatory work to be done for starting the scheme, duties and the responsibilities at various administrative levels, etc.

(xxii) The scheme should be sent to the Ministry of Education with a copy to the Adviser (Education), Planning Commission. This will be examined in the Ministry of Education in consultation with Planning Commission and Ministry of Finance. After the scheme is approved, Ministry of Education will release the grants in suitable instalments". (pp. 55-59)

Implementation of the Scheme

"National Programme of Nutritional Support to Primary Education" (commonly known as the Mid-day Meal Scheme) was launched as Centrally Sponsored Scheme on 15th August, 1995 by the then Prime Minister, P.V. Narasimha Rao. Its objective was to boost universalisation of primary education by increasing enrolment, retentions and attendance and simultaneously impacting on nutrition of students in primary classes. It involves provisions of lunch free of cost to school children in all working days. This scheme gives great relief to the parents who are economically poor and prepare to send children for work. This scheme was implemented in 2408 blocks in the first year and covered the whole country in a phased manner by 1997-98. The programme originally covered children of primary stage (Class I and V) in Government, local body and Government-aided schools, and was extended in October, 2002, to cover children studying in Education Guarantee Scheme (EGS) and Alternative and Innovative Education (AIE) Centres also. Government of India has now extended the benefit of the scheme up to the students of 7th standards. The Government of Tamil Nudu covers students up to 10th standard under the scheme with State Budget.

Provision of Central Assistance

Central assistance has been provided to State under the programme by way of: (i) Free supply of foodgrains from the nearest godown of Food Corporation of India (FCI) at the rate of 100 grams of wheat or rice per student per day (cost of which is reimbursed to Food Corporation of India by the Government of India), and (ii) Subsidy for transportation of foodgrains from FCI Depot to the Primary School, subject to a maximum of Rs. 75 per quintal. In addition, a Hill Transport Subsidy (HTS) is also admissible to States which are predominantly hilly, economically backward, and lack rail facilities, such as Arunachal Pradesh, Himachal Pradesh, Jammu and Kashmir, Manipur, Meghalaya, Nagaland, Mizoram, Sikkim and Tripura. In Hill States, FCI is responsible to deliver foodgrains at the nearest designated Principal Distribution Centres (PDCs). As per instructions of HTS, if FCI is unable to deliver foodgrains at the Principal Distribution Centres, it will issue foodgrains from the nearest designated Base Depots. In such cases, the actual cost of transportation of foodgrains from the nearest designated Principal Distribution Centres (PDCs) is reimbursed by FCI to the State/Union Territories as Hill Transport Subsidy.

Cost of Cooking

The cost of cooking of mid-day meal with free foodgrains includes such as cost of other ingredients, e.g. (1) pulses, vegetables, cooking oil and condiments, (2) cost of fuel, and (3) wages/remuneration payable to volunteers or amount to agency (e.g. Self-Help Group, Village Education Committee, School Monitoring-*cum*-Development Committee) responsible for cooking. As per the guidelines of the scheme the cooking cost need to be borne (a copy of Planning Commission's Circular dated 19.12.03) from the allocations of Pradhan Mantri Gramodaya Yojana (PMGY).

Infrastructure for the Scheme

The infrastructure like kitchen-*cum*-store, adequate water supply for drinking, cooking and washing purpose, cooking device (stove, *chullah*, etc.), containers for storage of foodgrains and other ingredients, utensils, etc. are expected to furnish by the State Governments or local bodies with their own funds or available under various Centrally Sponsored Schemes.

Revision of Scheme

Pursuant to the above, Central Government has approved a revised scheme, entitled "National Programme of Nutritional Support to Primary Education, 2004 (NP-NSPE, 2004)" whose main elements are as follows:

(1) Objectives of Revised Scheme

- To boost universalisation of primary education (Classes I-V) by improving enrolment, attendance, retention and learning levels of children especially those belonging to disadvantaged sections,
- To improve nutritional status of students of primary stage, and
- To provide nutritional support to students of primary stage, in drought affected areas during summer vacations also.

(2) Programme Intervention and Coverage

To achieve the above objectives, a cooked mid-day meal with minimum 300 calories and 8-12 grammes of protein content is provided to all children studying in Classes I-V in Government/local body and Government aided schools and

Education Guarantee Scheme (EGS) and Alternative Innovative Education (AIE). The State Government and Union Administration provide necessary infrastructure, logistic and financial support other than Central assistance to run the scheme effectively.

Central Assistance

Central Government provides assistance under the revised scheme to State Government/Union Territory Administrations to the following extent:

(1) Supply of free foodgrains (wheat/rice) @ 100 grams per child per school day from the nearest FCI godown.
(2) Reimbursement of actual cost incurred in transportation of foodgrains from nearest FCI godown to the primary school subject to the following ceiling:
  (a) Rs.100 per quintal for 11 special category States (viz. Arunachal Pradesh, Assam, Meghalaya, Mizoram, Manipur, Nagaland, Tripura, Sikkim, Jammu & Kashmir , Himachal Pradesh and Uttaranchal), and
  (b) Rs.75 per quintal for other States and Union Territories.
(3) Provide assistance for cooking cost at the following rates:
  (a) States in North Eastern Region: At the rate of Rs.1.80 per child per school day provided the State Government contributes a minimum of 20 paise.
  (b) For Other States and Union Territories at the rate of Rs. 1.50 per child per school day provided the State Government/UT Administration contribution a minimum of 50 paise.
  State Government/UT Administration will be required to provide the above minimum contribution in order to be eligible for the enhanced rate of Central assistance mentioned above.
  (c) Provide assistance for cooked mid-day meals during summer vacations to school children in

areas declared by State Government as drought affected.

(d) Provide assistance to construct kitchen-*cum*-store in a phased manner up to a maximum of Rs. 60,000 per unit. However, as allocations under scheme for construction of kitchen-*cum*-store for all schools in next 2-3 years may not be adequate. State would be expected to proactively pursue convergence with other development programmes for this purpose.

(e) Provide assistance in a phased manner for provisioning and replacement of kitchen devices at an average cost of Rs. 5,000 per school. States/ UT Administrations will have the flexibility to incur expenditure on the items listed below on the basis of the actual requirements of the school (provided that the overall average for the State/UT Administration remains Rs. 5,000 per school: (1) Cooking devices (Stove, *Chulha*, etc.), (2) Containers for storage of foodgrains and other ingredients, and (3) Utensils for cooking and serving.

(f) Provide assistance to State/Union Territories for Management, Monitoring and Evaluation (MME) at the rate of 1.8 per cent of total assistance on (a) free foodgrains, (b) transport cost, and (c) cooking cost. Another 0.2 per cent of the above amount will be utilized by the Central Government for Management, Monitoring and Evaluation.

Nodal Department at State and UT Levels

Every State Government/Union Territory Administration designates one of the departments as the Nodal Department for the programme. State Government can give responsibility of nodal department to any of the department, which can most effectively carry out nodal responsibility for effective implementation of the programme all over the State. (Many States have designed Department other than School

Education—e.g. Rural Development, Women and Child Development, Social Welfare, etc. as Nodal Department for the programme). State may set up a small Implementation Cell attached to the State Nodal Department to oversee the implementation of the programme by using a part of the funds for Management, Monitoring and Evaluation (MME).

District Level Nodal Department

Every State Government/UT Administration designates one nodal officer or agency at the district level (e.g. the District Collector, District Panchayat, etc.) which assigned overall responsibility of effective implementation of the programme at the district level.

Management at Local Level

At the local level State Government assigns responsibility for implementation and supervision of the programme to an appropriate body, e.g. Gram Panchayat, Municipality, Village Education Committee, Parent Teacher Association or School Management-*cum*-Development Committee. Responsibility for cooking is assigned to local women's Self-Help Group (SHGs), Youth Clubs affiliated to Nehru Yuvak Kendra (NYKs), Village Education Committee, School Development and Monitoring Committee, Parent Teacher Association/Mother Teacher Association, or prestigious Non-Governmental Organizations (NGOs) where available. Wherever women's SHG is not available then Village Education Committee/School Development-*cum*-Monitoring Committee, Parent-Teacher Association, Youth Club or an NGO can implement the programme by appointing part-time staff as cook, helper, etc. The preference need to be given to women belonging to Scheduled Castes and Scheduled Tribes. These organizations get foodgrains as thc parameters of the Scheme and other costs as per the State norms so that they can implement the programme in the assigned schools.

In urban areas, the choice has been given to the concerned organizations to prepare food in Centralized kitchen set up and the hot meal can be served to the schools under hygienic conditions through a reliable transport system. There are various organizations which follow such system popularly known as Naandi Foundation in Hyderabad-Secunderabad, International Society for Krishna Consciousness (ISKCON) in Bangalore and Tirupati, Kalahasti Temple Trust in Chittoor district of Andhra Pradesh, Sri Shakti in Ahmedabad, etc. supply cooked food to a large cluster of schools.

Allocation of Foodgrains to States, Districts and Schools

The Nodal Department will furnish to the Ministry by 15th of January every year district-wise request for allocation of foodgrains based on enrolment data of eligible Primary Schools and Education Guarantee Schools/Alternative and Innovative Education Centres, as on preceding 30th September, and anticipated enrolment in the next financial year.

Steering-cum-Monitoring Committees

To oversee the management and monitoring of the programme, Steering-*cum*-Monitoring Committees (SMCs) has been set up at various levels such as National, State, District, Taluk or Block, and Gram Panchayat with following functions :

(i) Guiding various implementation agencies,
(ii) Monitoring programme implementation, assessing its impact and taking corrective steps,
(iii) Making action on reports of independent monitoring/ evaluation agencies,
(iv) Effecting coordination and convergence among concerned department, agencies (e.g. FCI), and schemes, and
(v) Mobilizing community support and promoting public-private partnership for the programme.

National and State Level Steering-*cum*-Monitoring Committees (SMCs) are expected to meet at least once every six months whereas District and Block Level Steering-*cum*-Monitoring Committees need to meet at least once a quarter.

Coordination between Scheme and Education

It has to be always borne in mind that Mid-Day Meal programme is meant to boost children's participation and learning at the primary stage and not to interfere with it. The programme should not be implemented in such a manner that it in anyway, adversely affects either the duration or quality of actual teaching-learning in school. As a corollary, teachers should not be assigned responsibility connected with the programme except the following:

(i) testing of food prior to being served to children with a view to ensuring that it is of good quality, and is wholesome, and
(ii) supervision of actual serving and consumption of the mid-day meal so that it is done in an orderly manner, and children consume their meal hygienically.

Village Education Committees/Parent-Teacher Associations should make arrangements so that, as far as possible, at least two of their members are present everyday at the time of serving the meal, to shoulder above responsibilities, along with the teachers. The mid-day meal should be so organized that the entire process of serving and consumption of the meal does not take more than 30-40 minutes.

Voluntary Support by Community

Members of the community should be encouraged and invited to contribute towards providing a wholesome meal to children. There are many social occasions like religious festivals, marriages, death ceremony, etc. when local families will be happy to contribute a special dish or a sweet to the school mid-day meal programme. This, as also other voluntary contributions from the community (say in the form of cooking device/cooker, utensils, dairy products, fruits, vegetables, etc.) should be encouraged.

Role of Government for Elementary Education

To promote elementary education the Government of India has made provisions of free and compulsory education for all the children until they complete the age of 14 years under the Directive Principle of State Policy. Recognizing the need for literate populations and provisions of elementary education as a crucial input for nation building, the policy of the Government has been to provide free and compulsory education to all the children at least up to the elementary stage. The resolve was spelt out unequivocally and emphatically in the National Policy on Education (NPE), 1986 and the Programme of Actions (POA) 1992. The target for the VIII Five Year Plan has been divided into the following three broad parameters.

1. Universal Access

(i) Universal enrolment of all children including girls and boys belonging to Scheduled Caste and Scheduled Tribe,
(ii) Provision of primary school within one kilometre of walking distance and facility of non-formal education for school drop-outs, working children and girls who cannot attend formal schools, and
(iii) Improvement of ratio of upper primary to primary schools from existing 1:4 to 1:2.

2. Universal Retention

(iv) Reduction of drop-out rate between classes I to V, and I to VIII from the existing 46 per cent and 60 per cent to 20 per cent and 40 per cent respectively.

3. *Universal Achievement*

(v) Achievement of primary levels of learning by almost all children at the primary level and introduction of this concept at the upper primary stage". (4pp 15-23)

In favour of educational development, the Government of India has taken different initiatives timely along with implementation of mid-day meal scheme. Because of these efforts, the education in India has improved largely from 18.33 per cent in 1951 to 65.38 per cent in 2001 among all sections of the society. The following table shows general literacy rate in the country from last five decades.

Table 1.1: Population and literacy rate of Scheduled Castes and Scheduled Tribes

Sl. No.	Years	Population (in million)			Literacy (in %)		
		General	SC	ST	General	SC	ST
1.	1951	361.0	52	19	18.33	NA	NA
2.	1961	439.0	65	30	28.30	10.27	8.54
3.	1971	548.2	85	39	34.45	14.67	11.39
4.	1981	683.2	106	54	43.57	21.38	16.35
5.	1991	846.3	138	68	52.21	37.41	29.60
6.	2001	1027.0	167	84	65.38	54.69	47.10

NA: Not Available

Prior to mid-day meal scheme, the Government of India has initiated Operation Black Board Scheme in 1987 with the objective of to provide education through conducive manner so children get attraction towards education and enrolment could maintain constantly. In 1987 District Institutes of Educational Training (DIET) established across the country. The Andhra Pradesh Primary Education Project, Bihar Education Project, Uttar Pradesh Basic Education Project, Lok Jumbish and Shiksha Karmi Project of Rajasthan, District Primary Education Programme (DPEP), etc. were the main programmes which initiated between 1991 and 2001. The DPEP is presently under implementation in about 248 districts across the 18 States. In addition, the State Governments also initiated number of programmes. The success of these performances is partially reflected in primary enrolment which increased from 97 million in 1991 to 111 million in 1999; thus giving a rate of growth of 1.75 per cent per annum. The share of girls enrolment during the same period increased from 41.5 per cent to 43.5 per cent at the primary and 36.9 to 40.5 per cent at the upper primary level. To maintain attendance ratio high, Government of India has launched Sarva Shiksha Abhiyan which covers non-DPEP districts before the end of the Ninth Five Year Plan with focus on entire elementary level.

The elementary education in India has become one of the largest education systems in the World, providing accessibility of primary schools within the range of 1 kilometre walking distance whereas upper primary schools available with the range of 3 kilometres because of the institutions, the enrolment of students have increased to large extent. The following table shows enrolment status of students in India in different academic years.

Table 1.2: Enrolment of students in India

(*in millions*)

Sl. No.	Years	I-V		IV-VIII		Secondary/ Higher Secondary		Total	
		Boys	Girls	Boys	Girls	Boys	Girls	Boys	Girls
1	1950-51	13.8	5.4	2.6	0.5	1.3	0.2	17.7	6.1
2	1960-61	23.6	11.4	5.1	1.6	2.7	0.7	31.4	13.7
3	1970-71	35.7	21.3	9.4	3.9	5.7	1.9	50.8	27.1
4	1980-81	45.3	28.5	13.9	6.8	7.6	3.4	66.8	38.7
5	1990-91	57.0	40.4	21.5	12.5	12.8	6.3	91.3	59.2
6	2000-01	104.9	85.9	66.7	49.9	—	—	171.6	135.9

Sources: Selected Educational Statistics 2001-02, MHRD, GOI.

Despite all these efforts, the elementary education in India has not yet been accepted fully by the different social groups especially belonging to Scheduled Castes, Scheduled Tribes, nomadic tribes, semi-nomadic tribes, de-notified tribes, and economically deprived sections due to various reasons such as lack of educational environment or illiterate family background, poverty and economic constraints, poor infrastructure facilities in the educational institutions, apathetic treatment of teachers, development of industrialization and promotion of urbanizations, migration of parents, etc. are the some of the barriers for educational development. On the other side, far-flung location of schools, non-availability of transportation, lack of priority to the education, lack of link between education and employment, preference for households activities, attention for agriculture both in terms of their own field and on wage bases, care of siblings at home, persuasions of child labour, lack of motivation for education, prevalence of child marriage, attention for household or traditional occupations, expensive nature of education, responsibility of family, etc. are some of the reasons, which demotivate children and parents from educational development. The following table shows drop-out rates in school education at different levels.

Table 1.3: Drop out rates in different levels

(In per cent)

Sl. No.	Years	Primary			Elementary			Secondary		
		Boys	Girls	Total	Boys	Girls	Total	Boys	Girls	Total
1	1960-61	61.7	70.9	**66.0**	75.0	85.0	**80.1**	—	—	—
2	1970-71	64.5	70.9	**68.8**	74.6	83.3	**79.6**	—	—	—
3	1980-81	56.2	62.5	**60.0**	68.0	79.4	**72.8**	79.8	86.6	**85.0**
4	1990-91	40.1	46.0	**42.9**	59.1	65.1	**63.0**	67.5	76.9	**72.1**
5	2000-01	38.7	42.3	**41.2**	52.0	58.0	**55.5**	54.5	66.6	**58.5**
6	2001-02	38.4	39.9	**40.8**	52.9	56.9	**56.3**	64.2	68.6	**68.3**

Sources: Selected Educational Statistics—2001-02, p. 79, Department of Secondary and Higher Education, Ministry of Human Resource Development, GOI, New Delhi.

In present situation, India has got more than 6.0 lakh primary schools and 1.8 lakh upper primary schools where 15 crore students between the age of 6 and 14 years get education. 90.0 per cent rural population gets primary school within the range of 1 kilometre whereas 84.0 per cent of rural population gets accessibility of upper primary school within the range of

3 kilometres. India has got largest educational system in the World in terms of having highest students, teachers and educational systems but despite these achievements the drop-out rate is still higher compared to most of the countries. To prevent drop-out, Government of India commits that education is a right of each child. To promote education, the Government of India has launched Mid-Day Meals Scheme which ensures nutritional security of the child and keeps on tie with education.

The following table shows allocation of foodgrains throughout the country made by the Government of India between 2002-03 and 2006-07.

Table 1.4: Foodgrains Allocated and Lifted under Mid-Day Meal Scheme in States (2002-03 to 2006-07)

(Figures in Million Tonnes)

Sl. No.	State/ UT	Year	No. of children enrolled on 30th Sept. of the preceding year	Foodgrains allocated	Food-grains lifted	Per cent of lifting
1	2	3	4	5	6	7
1.	**Andhra Pradesh**	2002-03	7456254	223687.62	185620.15	82.98
		2003-04	7717673	178278.25	175513.12	98.45
		2004-05	9081299	213410.53	208218.16	97.57
		2005-06	6361814	114099.13	114099.11	100.00
		2006-07	6700878	131002.17	128652.73	98.21
2.	**Arunachal Pradesh**	2002-03	166637	4999.11	700.44	14.01
		2003-04	181606	5448.18	1209.40	22.20
		2004-05	177984	3559.68	3169.60	89.04
		2005-06	218905	4540.09	3559.96	78.41
		2006-07	218905	4558.70	3531.64	77.47
3.	**Assam**	2002-03	3149361	92545.89	43592.96	47.10
		2003-04	3210526	96315.78	78292.34	81.29
		2004-05	3387583	101627.49	87257.65	85.86
		2005-06	4795759	92125.70	75621.15	82.08
		2006-07	3525467	78617.92	48648.48	61.88
4.	**Bihar**	2002-03	8095780	242873.40	138678.82	57.10
		2003-04	8868044	245299.91	181362.17	73.93
		2004-05	9791760	195835.20	167153.54	85.35
		2005-06	12638429	218070.20	160939.69	73.80
		2006-07	12858653	248029.83	114728.22	46.26

(contd. Table 1.4)

(contd. Table 1.4)

Sl. No.	State/ UT	Year	No. of children enrolled on 30th Sept. of the preceding year	Foodgrains allocated	Food-grains lifted	Per cent of lifting
1	2	3	4	5	6	7
5.	**Chhattis-garh**	2002-03	2889116	74545.37	5531.31	7.42
		2003-04	2828582	56571.64	5642.11	9.97
		2004-05	2828582	56571.64	5380.09	9.51
		2005-06	2888868	53019.31	58485.09	110.31
		2006-07	3104573	69222.56	46379.82	67.00
6.	**Goa**	2002-03	68878	2066.34	0.00	0.00
		2003-04	69647	1253.65	0.00	0.00
		2004-05	68489	1232.80	0.00	0.00
		2005-06	67225	1411.73	1356.33	96.08
		2006-07	67686	1317.51	1317.51	100.00
7.	**Gujarat**	2002-03	3259341	65186.82	27551.01	42.26
		2003-04	3004496	60089.91	39533.12	65.79
		2004-05	3011034	60220.68	55083.21	91.47
		2005-06	5132959	67891.45	62107.16	91.48
		2006-07	3548712	75470.66	62522.18	82.84
8.	**Haryana**	2002-03	1538006	46140.18	41556.62	90.07
		2003-04	1578538	45871.00	41989.22	91.54
		2004-05	1627834	46075.44	20936.54	45.44
		2005-06	1645509	28672.99	14611.77	50.96
		2006-07	1612509	32895.18	17125.38	52.06
9.	**Himachal Pradesh**	2002-03	639974	19199.22	18777.33	97.80
		2003-04	614847	18445.41	17847.28	96.76
		2004-05	590351	17527.02	16926.82	96.58
		2005-06	577998	11447.25	11447.16	100.00
		2006-07	555378	12096.13	11394.55	94.20
10.	**Jammu & Kashmir**	2002-03	821890	24656.70	235.31	0.95
		2003-04	738777	22163.31	0.00	0.00
		2004-05	831215	24936.45	1662.69	6.67
		2005-06	1028425	18757.93	16653.87	88.78
		2006-07	1093613	20209.97	13168.28	65.16
11.	**Jhar-khand**	2002-03	2254066	51796.21	16548.37	31.95
		2003-04	2254066	51796.21	23039.70	44.48
		2004-05	3335485	83387.13	55467.28	66.52
		2005-06	4101554	82687.33	64552.50	78.07
		2006-07	4228353	84905.33	67154.41	79.09
12.	**Karnataka**	2002-03	5621960	153564.63	122262.01	79.62
		2003-04	5349540	145853.18	85386.97	58.54

(contd. Table 1.4)

(contd. Table 1.4)

Sl. No.	State/ UT	Year	No. of children enrolled on 30th Sept. of the preceding year	Foodgrains allocated	Food-grains lifted	Per cent of lifting
1	2	3	4	5	6	7
		2004-05	5126042	117558.08	87555.18	74.48
		2005-06	4962764	112863.57	82416.88	73.02
		2006-07	4653694	96517.61	83276.79	86.28
13.	**Kerala**	2002-03	2355686	47113.72	72409.04	153.69
		2003-04	2166510	43330.20	43329.20	100.00
		2004-05	2116354	42327.08	42327.08	100.00
		2005-06	1907000	28223.60	28223.60	100.00
		2006-07	2029411	32308.22	26915.28	83.31
14.	**Madhya Pradesh**	2002-03	7579750	212149.59	198003.28	93.33
		2003-04	7729652	165834.55	149768.56	90.31
		2004-05	7649784	159974.50	152011.18	95.02
		2005-06	8665342	191080.71	165648.99	86.69
		2006-07	8891737	188693.84	160166.41	84.88
15.	**Maharashtra**	2002-03	9930938	297928.14	218551.84	73.36
		2003-04	9721167	223586.84	183922.28	82.26
		2004-05	9665362	222303.33	150534.81	67.72
		2005-06	9779283	207809.77	134951.28	64.94
		2006-07	8147690	164135.22	148499.97	90.47
16.	**Manipur**	2002-03	287506	8625.18	8075.48	93.63
		2003-04	296211	8886.33	8881.02	99.94
		2004-05	305695	9170.85	9120.93	99.46
		2005-06	295096	6539.33	5914.25	90.44
		2006-07	295096	5665.84	5368.94	94.76
17.	**Meghalaya**	2002-03	434702	13041.06	11357.36	87.09
		2003-04	485980	10279.54	9373.40	91.19
		2004-05	502573	10051.46	9512.28	94.64
		2005-06	597555	10038.92	10041.42	100.02
		2006-07	627596	10543.61	9010.36	85.46
18.	**Mizoram**	2002-03	93608	2808.24	2246.59	80.00
		2003-04	94042	1880.84	1876.55	99.77
		2004-05	95619	1826.32	1829.66	100.18
		2005-06	104300	1837.86	1837.85	100.00
		2006-07	86504	1624.98	1743.98	107.32
19.	**Nagaland**	2002-03	159664	4789.92	4789.92	100.00
		2003-04	173598	5207.94	5082.53	97.59
		2004-05	173598	3471.96	3992.75	115.00
		2005-06	173598	3762.74	3506.53	93.19
		2006-07	173598	3541.40	3541.40	100.00

(contd. Table 1.4)

(contd. Table 1.4)

Sl. No.	State/ UT	Year	No. of children enrolled on 30th Sept. of the preceding year	Foodgrains allocated	Food-grains lifted	Per cent of lifting
1	2	3	4	5	6	7
20.	**Orissa**	2002-03	4621934	123762.01	105440.55	85.20
		2003-04	4631826	123424.87	114350.32	92.65
		2004-05	5151346	135293.02	105201.25	77.76
		2005-06	5156154	104110.32	86011.51	82.62
		2006-07	5002269	91938.20	80502.88	87.56
21.	**Punjab**	2002-03	1620811	48624.33	42099.50	86.58
		2003-04	1559682	45490.34	23707.95	52.12
		2004-05	1498697	43222.38	27886.73	64.52
		2005-06	1552404	28053.43	7821.01	27.88
		2006-07	1488412	29401.81	22761.08	77.41
22.	**Rajasthan**	2002-03	7177718	157909.79	14154.12	8.96
		2003-04	7678153	168919.37	136487.45	80.80
		2004-05	7662192	168568.22	121027.06	71.80
		2005-06	10215570	196108.30	122477.08	62.45
		2006-07	7335359	133312.81	96532.6	72.41
23.	**Sikkim**	2002-03	77033	2310.99	2042.70	88.39
		2003-04	76828	1536.56	1296.26	84.36
		2004-05	83602	1672.04	1657.24	99.11
		2005-06	98000	2126.59	2126.59	100.00
		2006-07	102520	1960.70	1880.28	95.90
24.	**Tamil Nadu**	2002-03	5401644	108032.88	80000.25	74.05
		2003-04	5529945	110598.90	79654.67	72.02
		2004-05	4305932	86118.64	71997.91	83.60
		2005-06	4152167	76586.73	69395.56	90.61
		2006-07	3909913	73115.37	65203.65	89.18
25.	**Tripura**	2002-03	459981	13799.43	10069.21	72.97
		2003-04	453854	9077.08	8906.40	98.12
		2004-05	458020	9160.40	9053.71	98.84
		2005-06	525645	9882.13	9429.86	95.42
		2006-07	520610	10787.04	5183.03	48.05
26.	**Uttara-khand**	2002-03	821507	24645.21	15206.34	61.70
		2003-04	787193	15743.86	19781.88	125.65
		2004-05	811204	16224.08	14181.57	87.41
		2005-06	779596	14180.85	13622.47	96.06
		2006-07	779826	14535.96	14002.23	96.33
27.	**Uttar Pradesh**	2002-03	14855697	445670.91	405310.57	90.94
		2003-04	16374892	491246.76	365300.77	74.36
		2004-05	16996916	509907.48	452280.03	88.70

(contd. Table 1.4)

(contd. Table 1.4)

Sl. No.	*State/ UT*	*Year*	*No. of children enrolled on 30th Sept. of the preceding year*	*Foodgrains allocated*	*Food-grains lifted*	*Per cent of lifting*
1	*2*	*3*	*4*	*5*	*6*	*7*
		2005-06	18644467	335973.30	285077.65	84.85
		2006-07	14728060	346109.28	257665.51	74.45
28.	**West Bengal**	2002-03	9764184	292925.43	230524.86	78.70
		2003-04	10268683	305987.74	255689.48	83.56
		2004-05	10326600	302571.85	264088.41	87.28
		2005-06	10886311	205424.69	175974.72	85.66
		2006-07	9247449	174499.36	155648.02	89.20
29.	**Andaman & Nicobar Islands**	2002-03	35886	1076.58	1018.67	94.62
		2003-04	35179	703.58	703.58	100.00
		2004-05	35186	774.09	774.09	100.00
		2005-06	34517	668.25	533.98	79.91
		2006-07	34107	575.73	551.87	95.86
30.	**Chandigarh**	2002-03	41720	1251.60	554.78	44.33
		2003-04	42520	977.96	543.98	55.62
		2004-05	42366	974.42	682.44	70.04
		2005-06	56500	1007.96	900.45	89.33
		2006-07	59993	1228.66	524.75	42.71
31.	**Dadar & Nagar Haveli**	2002-03	26004	780.12	379.69	48.67
		2003-04	29480	678.04	393.20	57.99
		2004-05	30176	603.52	429.06	71.09
		2005-06	33454	610.20	457.17	74.92
		2006-07	32251	508.15	455.2	89.58
32.	**Daman & Diu**	2002-03	15214	304.28	233.68	76.80
		2003-04	15163	303.26	198.24	65.37
		2004-05	15187	303.74	234.60	77.24
		2005-06	15300	302.94	191.11	63.09
		2006-07	13539	246.14	190.96	77.58
33.	**Delhi**	2002-03	1010919	20218.38	3802.55	18.81
		2003-04	1036711	21739.06	7259.90	33.40
		2004-05	1078241	21564.82	14661.62	67.99
		2005-06	1238188	20165.55	17507.03	86.82
		2006-07	1116492	19579.14	16077.15	82.11
34.	**Lakshadweep**	2002-03	0	0.00	0.00	0.00
		2003-04	0	0.00	0.00	0.00
		2004-05	0	0.00	0.00	0.00
		2005-06	0	0.00	0.00	0.00
		2006-07	10430	183.57	0.00	0.00

(contd. Table 1.4)

(contd. Table 1.4)

Sl. No.	State/ UT	Year	No. of children enrolled on 30th Sept. of the preceding year	Foodgrains allocated	Food-grains lifted	Per cent of lifting
1	2	3	4	5	6	7
35.	**Pondicherry**	2002-03	62349	1247.00	736.23	59.04
		2003-04	62349	1246.98	2130.12	170.82
		2004-05	53221	1064.42	1027.95	96.57
		2005-06	50723	879.54	812.83	92.42
		2006-07	55200	1013.47	917.21	90.50
Total	**All India**	2002-03	102795718	2830276.28	2028061.52	71.66
		2003-04	105665960	2684067.03	2068453.19	77.06
		2004-05	108915529	2669090.76	2163323.12	81.05
		2005-06	119381379	2250960.37	1808313.61	80.34
		2006-07	106856483	2160352.08	1671242.96	77.36

Source: Report No. PA 13 of 2008 of the Comptroller and Auditor General of India.

Objectives of the Study

- To understand the variance of administrative structure for implementation of the scheme in different states and comparative effectiveness of the structure,
- To examine the extent of involvement and contribution of various level institutions in implementation of the scheme,
- To examine the problems in proper implementation of the scheme, and
- To make suitable suggestions for further improvement in functioning of the scheme.

Methodology

This study has been carried out in two consecutive years, i.e. 2006-07 and 2007-08. In 2006-07, Tamil Nadu, Gujarat and Himachal Pradesh were selected whereas in 2007-08, Andhra Pradesh, Uttar Pradesh and West Bengal were chosen. In Tamil

Nadu, Uthirameruru and Thirupurar blocks of Kanchipuram district were selected whereas in Gujarat, Himatnagar and Bhiloda of Sabarkanta districts were chosen. In Himachal Pradesh, Gumarwin I and Gumarwin II of Bilaspur district were selected. In each district two blocks (in case of Gujarat—taluk) were chosen. Further, from each district, 20 schools were chosen which means total 60 schools were taken in sample from the three states.

In 2007-08, the sample size has been increased from 20 to 60 with consistence of 20 schools reason-wise. The logic behind this was to understand function of the scheme region-wise because each state has its geographical and cultural variation. Keeping in view, the samples have been drawn region-wise in Andhra Pradesh, Uttar Pradesh and West Bengal.

In Andhra Pradesh, Valigonda mandal of Nalgonda district (Telangana region), Baptla mandal of Guntur district (Coastal region) and Irala mandal of Chittoor district (Rayalaseema) were chosen. Similarly, in Uttar Pradesh, Behjam block of Lakhimpur Kheri district, Soran block of Allahabad district and Chirgaon block of Jhansi district were chosen. In West Bengal, Barrackpur II, Kanksa and Ratua blocks were chosen simultaneously from North 24 Parganas, Burdwan and Malda districts. The selection of schools, blocks and districts were made based on performance of the scheme and impact of the scheme region-wise. Table 1.5 shows samples (number of schools) covered state-wise.

This study covers different aspects like functions of the committees which constituted at state, district, block and gram panchayat level. On the other side, this study concentrates on role and functions of nodal department especially at grassroots level where this scheme has been implementing. This study focuses on monitoring mechanism of the scheme along with other relevant issues like availability of infrastructural facilities in the school premises, coverage of enrolment, retention, drops out and result of the students from last five years to understand the function and impact of the scheme.

In the study, schools located in tribal areas were also taken in sample. This scheme has been implemented widely throughout the country which is world's largest school children feeding programme. Under Swarnjayanti Gram Rojgar Yojana (SGRY) funds were allocated for construction of the kitchen sheds but now the SGRY is replaced by Mahatma Gandhi National Rural Employment Guarantee Scheme (MGNREGS) since October 2009.

The following table shows samples (schools) mandal/ block, district/region and state-wise.

Table 1.5 (a): Number of schools covered year-wise in 2006-07

Sl. No.	*State*	*District*	*Block*	*Sample Size (Schools)*
1.	Tamil Nadu	Kanchipuram	1. Uthirameruru	10
			2. Thirupurar	10
2.	Gujarat	Sabarkanta	1. Himatnagar	10
			2. Bhiloda	10
3.	Himachal Pradesh	Bilaspur	1. Gumarwin I	10
			2. Gumarwin II	10
	Total			**60**

Table 1.5 (b): Number of schools covered year-wise in 2007-08

Sl. No.	*State*	*District/Region*	*Mandal/block*	*Sample Size (Schools)*
1.	Andhra Pradesh	Nalgonda (Telangana)	1. Valigonda	20
		Baptla (Coastal)	2. Guntur	20
		Irla (Rayalaseema)	3. Chittoor	20
2.	Uttar Pradesh	Lakhimpur Kheri	1. Behjam	20
		Allahabad	2. Soran	20
		Jhansi	3. Chirgaon	20
3.	West Bengal	North 24 Parganas	1. Barrackpur II	20
		Burdwan	2. Kanksa	20
		Malda	3. Tatua	20
	Total			**180**

In Andhra Pradesh, Mandals have been created after bifurcation the blocks to make accessible Government machineries to the people. A Mandal is smaller than block area and population-wise which introduced by the former Chief Minister of Andhra Pradesh N.T. Rama Rao when Telugu-desham party was in power. Mandal headquarters in general accessible to the rural people.

Note : Gujarat follows taluk system whereas Andhra Pradesh follows Mandal system. The rest of studied states follow concept of block system which is bottom unit of administrations set up.

2

Administrative Structure

Tamil Nadu

The provision of Mid Day Meal Scheme in Tamil Nadu first of all began in 1923 for disadvantaged children in Madras Municipality Corporation. It was restarted in 1960 by the then Chief Minister, K. Kamraj in some pockets of the state. But the major thrust came in 1982 when and then the Chief Minister of Tamil Nadu, Dr. M.G. Ramachandran decided to universalize the scheme for all children in Government schools in primary classes. Since 1st July, 1982 in rural areas and later on with narrow gap this scheme had been extended in urban areas on 15th September, 1982 and thereafter this scheme has become part of educational system. This scheme was launched based on nutrition surveys which revealed that energy in-take of children in the low income group is inadequate, very much shorter and lighter in-take, vitamin A deficiency and anemia noticed and impairs learning ability and school performance. Initially this scheme was launched with the help of World Bank assistance.

Now this scheme has been expended for the students of VI to X classes. But expenditure beyond primary level is borne by State Government. The Noon Meals Programme is named as Puratchi Thaaivar MGR Nutritious Programme. During 2006-07, this scheme had been running in 41,344 schools (which are popularly known Centres in official terms) benefiting 58.75 lakhs of students. This scheme covers all those schools where minimum 25 children enrolled. There is no upper ceiling in strength of the students. All those who are willing to take food in the school the scheme cover them. The strength of beneficiaries (children who avail the benefit of the scheme popularly known beneficiaries in official terms) decides in the beginning of the academic year, and then if there is any change in enrolment later stage then prior permission of Block Development Officer is required.

The Government of Tamil Nadu runs this scheme throughout the year for pre-schooling and primary school children (up to 5th standard) whereas for the students of 6th to 10th standard this scheme provides food for 220 days. The Government of India provides foodgrains and financial assistance for 200 days up to primary level children. The following table shows feeding scale age group-wise in Tamil Nadu:

Table 2.1: Feeding scale age group-wise in Tamil Nadu

Commodity	*2-5 years*	*5-9 years*	*10-13 years*	*14-15 years*
Rice	80 gm	100 gm	100 gm	120 gm
Dal	10 gm	15 gm	15 gm	15 gm
Oil	2 gm	1 gm	1 gm	1 gm
Vegetable & condiments	35 paise	35 paise	35 paise	35 paise

In addition to above, one boiled egg is provided to each child on every Monday and Wednesday with 20 grams of black Bengal gram or 20 gram of Green gram on each Thursday including 20 grams of boiled potato on every Friday. The above quantity fulfils following nutritional values.

Table 2.2: Nutritional assessment of diet for the children

Commodity	*Calorific value*	*Protein content*
Rice	340	800
Pulses	50	3.20
Vegetables	30	1.00
Egg (2 per week)	22.7	1.70
Black Bengal gram/green gram	9.9	0.59
Potato	2.8	0.05
Oil	9.0	0.00
Pending intake per student	464.4	14.54
Government of India's norms (Minimum)	450.0	12.00

Chart: Supply of Foodgrains in the State of Tamil Nadu

Rice	*Commodities Dal, gram and Oil*	*Salt*
Food Corporation of India, Godown	Tamil Nadu Civil Supply Corporation (TNCSC), Chennai godown	Tamil Nadu Salt Corporation
TNCSC Taluka godown	TNCSC Taluk godowns	TNCSC District godowns
Noon Meal Centres	Noon Meal Centres	TNCSC Taluk godowns

Note: These commodities normally supply during 10-25 of each month. The process of local audit takes place once in a year.

In Tamil Nadu, this scheme transfers from one to other department due to political interference between two major parties such as All India Anna Dravida Munnetra Kazhagam (AIADMK) and Dravida Munnetra Kazhagam (DMK). When and then AIADMK comes into the power this scheme runs by the State Rural Development Department whereas when and then DMK comes into the power this scheme runs by State Social Welfare Department. Over the years, this scheme has been implemented through various departments like:

- Education Department from 1982 to May 1990
- Rural Development Department from June 1990 to September 1992
- Social Welfare Department from October 1992 to September 1997
- Rural Development Department from October 1997 to July 2006
- Social Welfare Department from August 2006 till date.

In Tamil Nadu, Organizers work in the State Government Scale of 600-10-720-20-1100 whereas Cooks get consolidated amount of Rs.1,300 per month. Similarly, helper gets consolidated amount of Rs.1,000 per month. One additional cook and assistant to cook is also provided to such Centres where strength of the students reaches beyond five hundred.

Chart: Flow of Fund for the Scheme in Tamil Nadu

Government of India		
Government of Tamil Nadu		
District, Social Welfare	Commissioner, Municipal Administration	Commissioner, Civil Supply
District Collector	District Collector	District Collector,(Except Chennai and Commissioner, Municipality Administration)
Block Development Officer (BDO)	Municipality Commissioner	TNCSC
Noon Meal Centre	Noon Meal Centre	—
Noon Meal Organizer	Noon Meal Organizer	
Fund Utilizes for	**Fund Utilizes for**	**Fund Utilizes for**
Salary Grant	Salary Grant	Rice
Purchase of vegetables, eggs, vessels, plates, tumblers, stationery	Purchase of vegetables, eggs, vessels, plates, tumblers, stationery	Dal and Oil

The following chart shows administrative set up in Tamil Nadu for implementation of the scheme.

Chart : Steering-*cum*-Monitoring Committees at various levels

Sl. No.	*Name of the Committee*	*Members with Status*
1	State Level Steering-*cum*-Monitoring Committee	Under Chairmanship of Chief Secretary
2	District Level Steering-*cum*-Monitoring Committee	Under Chairmanship of District Collector
3	Block Level Steering-*cum*-Monitoring Committee	Headed by Block Development Officer
4	Panchayat Level Steering-*cum*-Monitoring Committee	Headed by President (Gram Panchayat)

Note: All these committees monitor the scheme and make suitable changes

Each committee comprises members of different background such as officials, experts of subject, social activists, leaders, self-help group, etc. The following chart highlights the structure of each committee constituted from State to Gram Panchayat levels.

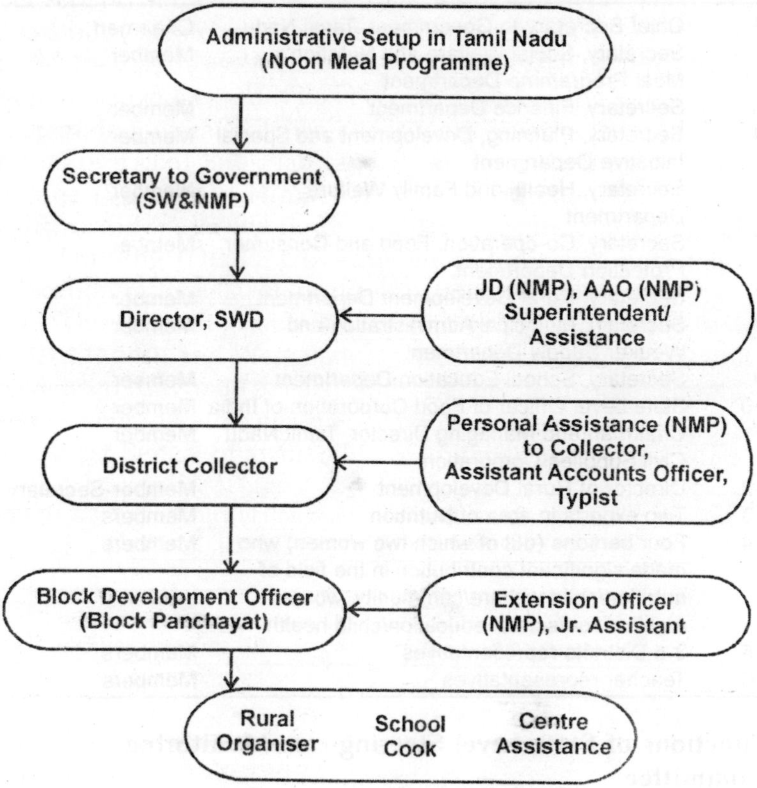

This committee has been functioning w.e.f. 23rd February, 2006, (1) Member from category 13 to 16 nominated by the Chairman for two years or till the nominations of their successors whichever is later. (2) This committee decides weekly menu for students of all classes (i.e. I-V, VI-X). (3) The members of the committee expected to meet at least once in six months but Director Social Welfare Department (Member Secretary) review the progress of the scheme once in three or four weeks. Director, Social Welfare Department also organizes meeting with PA to Collector (Noon Meal Programme) to review the scheme. In this meeting the State Minister also participates.

Chart : State Level Steering-*cum*-Monitoring Committee in Tamil Nadu

Sl. No.	*Designation of the Officers*	*Status*
1.	Chief Secretary to Government, Tamil Nadu	Chairman
2.	Secretary, Social Welfare and Nutrition's Meal Programme Department	Member
3.	Secretary, Finance Department	Member
4.	Secretary, Planning, Development and Special Initiative Department	Member
5.	Secretary, Health and Family Welfare Department	Member
6.	Secretary, Co-operation, Food and Consumer Protection Department	Member
7.	Secretary, Rural Development Department	Member
8.	Secretary, Municipal Administration and Weaker Supply Department	Member
9.	Secretary, School Education Department	Member
10.	State Level Officer of Food Corporation of India	Member
11.	Chairman and Managing Director, Tamil Nadu Civil Supplies Corporation	Member
12.	Director of Rural Development	Member-Secretary
13.	Two experts in area of Nutrition	Members
14.	Four persons (out of which two women) who made significant contribution in the field of nutrition/child welfare/community, women mobilization/school education/child health	Members
15.	3-5 Districts representatives	Members
16.	Teacher representatives	Members

Functions of State Level Steering-*cum*-Monitoring Committee

1. Guiding various implementation agencies,
2. Monitor programme implementation, assessing its impact, and taking corrective steps,
3. Taking action on reports of independent monitoring/ education agencies,
4. Effective coordination and convergence among departments, agencies (e.g. Food Corporation of India) and scheme,
5. Mobilizing community and promoting public private partnership for the programme, and

6. This committee will meet at least once in every six months.

This committee makes changes in menu timely and enhance amount to maintain quality of food so that students would not get repeated food. The following menu is being followed presently with the recommendations of this committee.

Chart : Menu in Tamil Nadu

Days	*Types of food supply*
Monday	Rice, Dal with vegetables, and one egg
Tuesday	Rice and Dal
Wednesday	Rice, Dal with vegetables, and one egg
Thursday	Rice, Dal, Black Bengal gram or Green Gram (20 gms)
Friday	Rice, Dal and boiled potato 20 gms

In Tamil Nadu, some of the schools also run on Saturday for small children to encourage them for education. On Saturday they get Rice, Dal and Vegetables. In Tamil Nadu, this scheme is influenced by the ruling parties and accordingly one or other party promotes intake of eggs weekly, therefore, sometimes suppliers find difficulty to supply required quantum of eggs.

Administrative Set-up at District Level

Chart : District Level Steering-*cum*-Monitoring Committee in Tamil Nadu

Sl. No.	*Designation of the Officer*	*Status*
1.	District Collector	Chairman
2.	District Revenue Officer	Member
3.	Commissioner of Municipal Corporation/Municipalities	Member
4.	Personal Assistance (General) to Collector	Member
5.	Additional Personal Assistant to Collector	Member
6.	Deputy Director (Grievance Day)	Member
7.	District Supply Officer (Petitions)	Member
8.	District Adi-Dravidan Welfare Officer	Member
9.	District Backward Classes Welfare Officer	Member
10.	Assistant Commissioner (Excise)	Member

(Contd.)

Sl. No.	*Designation of the Officer*	*Status*
11.	Divisional Officers	Member
12.	Revenue Tahsildar	Member
13.	Taluk Supply Officer	Member
14.	Other P.A. to Collector	Member
15.	Project Officer of DRDAs	Member
16.	Project Officer, Women Development Corporation (WDC)	Member
17.	Personal Assistance (Project Director) to Collector	Member
18.	Assistant Director (Parent Teacher Association)	Member
19.	Assistant Director (Audit)	Member
20.	Personal Assistant (Noon Meal Programme) to Collector	Member-Secretary
21.	Joint Director (Medical)	Member
22.	Deputy Director (Health)	Member
23.	Corporation/Municipal/Health Officer	Member
24.	Assistant Project Officer/Project Officer (District Rural Development Agency)	Member
25.	Assistant Project Officer/Project Officer, WDC	Member

All members supposed to visit at least two centres in a month and check the quality of food, make verification of stock, advice to maintain clean or hygienic environment, sanitation, etc. If they find any deficiency, then discuss in meeting or they bring to the notice of District Collector.

Chart : Block Level Steering-*cum*-Monitoring Committee in Tamil Nadu

Sl. No.	*Designation of the Officer*	*Status*
1.	Block Development Officer	Chairman
2.	Deputy Block Development Officer	Member
3.	Extension Officer	Member
4.	Rural Welfare Officer	Member
5.	Revenue Inspector	Member

All members need to visit centres frequently during 12.00 noon—1.00 pm and inform to Block Development Officer, General (BDO General).

These members are supposed to visit centres and check the quantity and quality of the food which are supplied to the students including cleanliness, healthy environment, etc. and make suitable suggestions for further improvement.

Chart : Panchayat Level Steering-*cum*-Monitoring Committee in Tamil Nadu

Sl. No.	*Designation of the Officer*	*Status*
1.	Panchayat President	President
2.	Head Master	Member-Secretary
3.	Village Administrative Officer	Member
4.	Woman from Self-Help Group	Member
5.	Student's mother	Member
6.	Parent Teacher Association (Male)	Member

Gujarat

Gujarat is one of the pioneer states to introduce the concept of providing hot cooked mid-day meals to all the children from class I to VII in Government, Municipal Corporations and local bodies' schools. By the mid of 1980s, Gujarat had universalized a Cooked Mid-Day Meal Programme with their own resources for children studying at the primary level stage then this scheme was discontinued from August 1990 to October 1991 and replaced by Free for Education Programme wherein children with 70 per cent attendance were provided 10 kg of foodgrains free of cost. Mid-day Meals Scheme was reintroduced on 15th January, 1992 in the State in its original form. Since August 1995, this scheme has been running with the assistance of Government of India but beyond the primary level (i.e. for upper primary classes) the expenditure is borne by the State Government.

Table 2.3: Feeding scale student-wise in Gujarat

Commodities	*Quantity*
Wheat/rice	100 grams
Pulses	20 grams
Vegetable and condiments	50 grams
Edible oil	10 grams
Total	**180 grams equivalent to 450 calories**

In 2006-07, this scheme was running in around 30,000 centres covering more than 35 lakh students. As per Supreme Court Direction, Mid-Day Meal Centres are required to be continued for minimum 200 days in each academic year. Chief Secretary has given instructions to all Collectors and District Development Officers and Municipal Commissioners by Video Conference on 23rd July, 2003 for Tithi Bhojan (provide by the community) to the children availing mid-day meal in the schools. In this programme donation from public is required to run mid-day meal centres for particular day and on that day children of the schools will get food in form of donation by the community.

Table 2.4: Feeding scale cost per child in Gujarat

Sl. No.	*Commodities*	*Amount*
1.	Foodgrains	0.80
2.	Vegetables, condiments and fuel	0.70
3.	Administrative expenditure	0.25
	Total	**1.75**

Apart from the Government mechanism, the scheme is run by a non-Governmental Organization (NGO), namely: Sri Shakti, which is located in Ahmedabad. This NGO covers 477 schools within the radius of 30 km. The Government of India provides foodgrains and financial assistance at Rs. 2.0 per student per school day. This NGO manages convergence cost and transportation cost out of above assistance which is given by the Government based on strength of the students school-wise. This NGO has employed 100 persons of which women employees are more who take care for cleaning the foodgrains, cooking, and cleaning the vessels.

The following chart shows distribution of food grains in Gujarat.

Chart : Foodgrains Supply in Gujarat

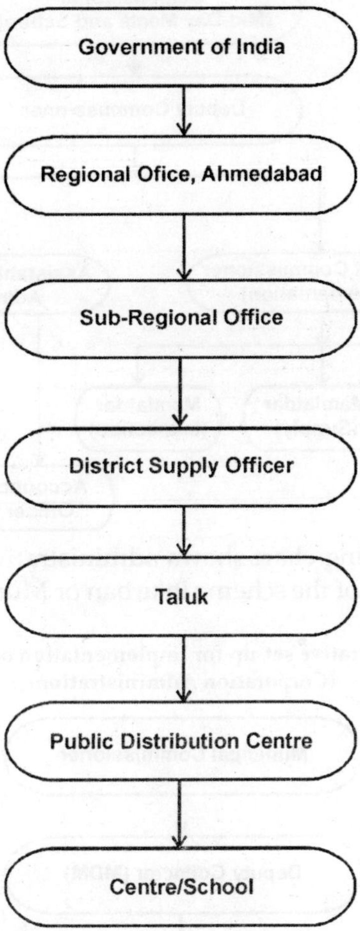

The Government of India supplies foodgrains and convergence cost of Rs. 1.50 per student per school day whereas Government of Gujarat contributes 70 paisa in case of each student each day. Unlike Tamil Nadu, the Government of Gujarat is not supplying oil, salt, condiments, etc., which responsibility has been given to the centres to purchase.

The following chart shows administrative set-up for the implementation of the scheme in rural areas of Gujarat.

Administrative set-up for Implementation of the Scheme in Gujarat

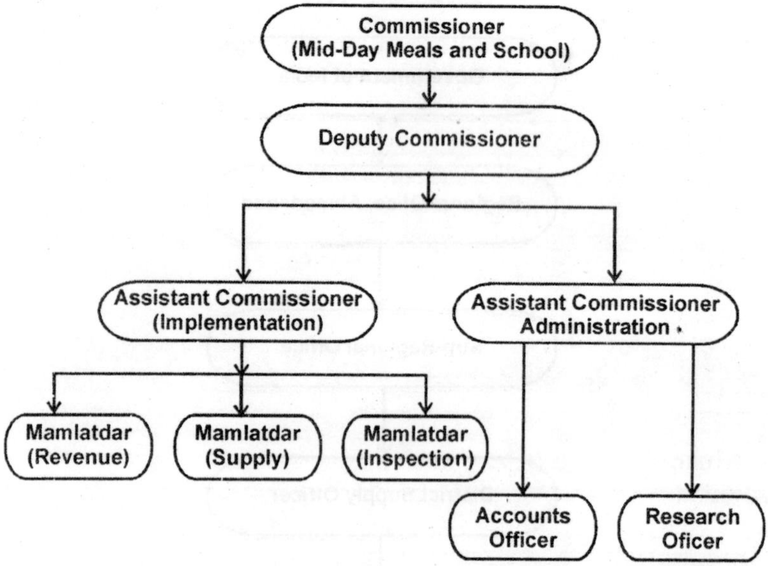

The following chart shows administrative set-up for the implementation of the scheme in urban or Municipal localities.

Administrative set-up for Implementation of Scheme (Corporation Administration)

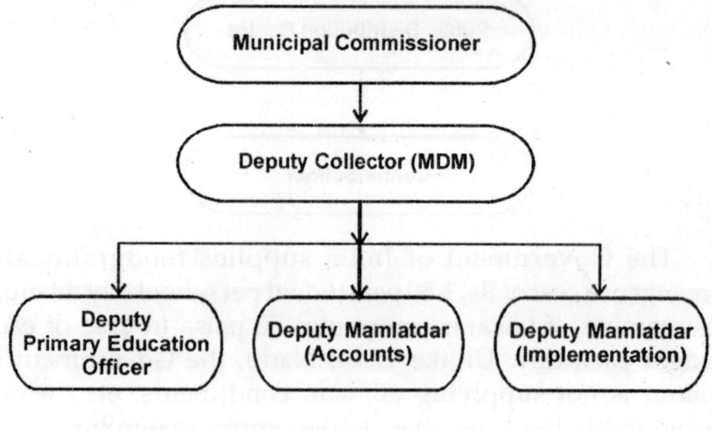

Gujarat comprises 25 districts. The similar nature of menu has been implemented throughout the state but flexibility has been given to the district authorities to follow the same menu according to their wish for example Monday's menu can be followed on Wednesday. The following chart highlights the menu of Sabarkanta district of the State which was chosen for study.

Chart : Weekly Menu in Sabarkanta District

Days	*Types of food supply*
Monday	Vegetarian pulav
Tuesday	Muthia (local dish)
Wednesday	Dal dhokli (local dish) and rice
Thursday	Sweet upma/lapsi/sukdi
Friday	Dal dhokli
Saturday	Vegetarian pulav

In addition to the cooked food, the State Government also provides a package of Micro Nutrient Therapeutic Medicines like Vitamin A for improvement of eye-sight and removal of night blindness, tablet Albendazol for deworming and tablet Ferrous Sulphate as iron booster to all the students to sustain and increase the health standard along with nutritional standards. This medicinal package has been widely acclaimed by Government of India, United Nations International Children Emergency Fund (UNICEF) and World Health Organization (WHO). This facility meets an expenditure of Rs. 4.0 crore per annum. All these facilities have been implemented from 1993.

The Government of Gujarat has taken following steps such as : (1) This menu has been implemented from December 2006, (2) The ingredient of food contains 100 grams rice or wheat, 20 grams dal, 7 grams oil, 50 grams vegetables, and condiment, etc. (3) Government has constructed 12752 kitchen-*cum*-store rooms under SGRY, Tribal Sub-Plan, etc. Now construction is being implemented under Gujarat Bal Nidhi Fund, (4) The range of employee (on consolidated salary) determined on following criteria: one cook and one helper is given where strength exists up to 250 students, one cook and two helpers are being provided where enrolment registered between 251 and 500 students, two cooks and two helpers are provided where enrolment is between 501 and 750 students, and wherever more than 750 students enrolled two cooks and three helpers are being given for smooth functioning of cooking and supply of food.

The following tables show physical structure of Steering-*cum*-Monitoring Committees at various levels from State to Panchayat covering different officials, representatives and experts.

Chart : State Level Steering-*cum*-Monitoring Committee in Gujarat

Sl. No.	*Designation of the Officer*	*Status*
1.	Chief Secretary to Government, Gujarat	Chairman
2.	Principal Secretary, School Education	Member
3.	Secretary, Rural Development	Member
4.	Secretary, Urban Development	Member
5.	Secretary, Finance Department	Member
6.	Secretary, Planning Commission	Member
7.	Secretary, Food and Civil Supply	Member
8.	Secretary, Women and Child Development	Member
9.	State Level Officer, Food Corporation of India	Member
10.	Secretary, Health and Family Welfare	Member
11.	Secretary, Municipal Administration	Member
12.	Commissioner, Mid-day meal, School	Member-Secretary
13.	Two experts in the area of nutrition	Members
14.	Four (of two at least women) significant contribution in nutrition, child welfare education, health, etc	Members
15.	3-5 districts representatives	Member
16.	1 Teacher representative	Member

The State Level Committee discusses issues like to fulfil requirements of foodgrains in time from Government of India, release sanction of advance, repairing of kitchen sheds or guide appropriate for kitchen shed, make arrangement of inspecting centres, replace or sanction advance for vessels, recommend for revision of salary, honorarium, etc. timely.

Chart : District Level Steering-*cum*-Monitoring Committee in Sabarkanta District

Sl. No.	*Designation of the Officer*	*Status*
1.	District Collector	Chairman
2.	Deputy Collector, Mid-Day Meal (MDM)	Member-Secretary
3.	District Education Officer (Primary)	Member
4.	District Development Officer	Member
5.	District Supply Officer	Member
6.	Chief District Health Officer	Member
7.	President, Municipality	Member
8.	Child Welfare Activists (4)	Members
9.	Principal of Home Science	Member
10.	Sitting members of Taluka (2)	Members
11.	Teacher Representatives (4)	Members

For review the performance of the scheme, Executive and District Coordinating Committee organizes meetings on every third Wednesday. This meeting is held at District Headquarters.

Chart : Taluk Level Steering-*cum*-Monitoring Committee in Sabarkanta District

Sl. No.	*Designation of the Officer*	*Status*
1.	Sub-Divisional Magistrate	Chairman
2.	Taluk Revenue Officer	Member-Secretary
3.	Taluk Development Officer	Member
4.	Medical Officer (Primary Health Centre)	Member
5.	Education Inspector	Member
6.	Taluk Godown Manager	Member
7.	President, Municipality	Member
8.	Sarpanchs (4)	Members
9.	Teachers (1)	Member

At Taluk level the issues related to the scheme discussed in review meeting which is held on 5th of every month.

Chart : Panchayat Level Monitoring Committee in Sabarkanta District

Sl. No.	Designation of the Officer	Status
1.	President, Gram Panchayat	President
2.	Principal/School Head Master	Member-Secretary
3.	Organizer	Member
4.	Four village prestigious persons out of which two women	Members

This Committee also gives instructions to school head masters/head mistress to keep foodgrains and other relevant commodities in the school premises, organize meeting at least once in a month, and keep vigilance whether students are involved in preparation of the food, monitoring of girls enrolment, etc.

Himachal Pradesh

The Mid-Day Meal Scheme in Himachal Pradesh was launched on 15th August, 1995 with twin objectives: (1) Boosting universalization of primary education by increasing enrolment, retention and attendance, and (2) By positively impacting on Nutritional Status of children studying in Class I-V in the Primary schools. This scheme was launched in a phased manner in the state and uncooked foodgrains (rice) at the rate of 3 kg per month per student were provided to the children of classes I to V with 80 per cent attendance for 10 academic months in all the Government/Government aided primary schools of entire state till the May 2003. In the first phase 13 Community Development Blocks, in second phase 33 Community Development Blocks, and finally, in third phase, all the 72 Community Development blocks were covered under the scheme.

Consequent upon the orders of Hon'ble Supreme Court of India, Government of Himachal Pradesh decided to provide a supplementary meal which is protein rich, nutritionally balanced with appropriate micro nutrients and iodized salt, etc. so as to enhance the child learning ability in order to achieve the targeted objectives, as envisaged in the scheme as every working day, to the student of Government and Government aided primary schools of the state in a phased manner.

In the 1st phase, all the 583 Governments and Government aided primary schools which falls under scheduled area covered. These areas covered 43 per cent of geographical area of the state. In these areas the Hot Cooked Food began to provide since May 2003. The prior to Hot Cooked Meal, students were getting foodgrains of 3 kg which has been increased up to 10 kg between August 1995 and August 2004. This facility was provided in Government and Government aided primary schools throughout the state. Teachers used to go with the students at the fair price shop and helping then to get foodgrains. But from September 2004 onwards students are getting cooked meals in the centres. The following table shows feeding scale both in tribal and non-tribal areas of Himachal Pradesh.

Table 2.5 : Feeding Scale in Tribal and Non-tribal areas in Himachal Pradesh

Sl. No.	*Commodities/Ingredient*	*Tribal Areas*	*Non-tribal Areas*
1.	Rice	100	100 grams
2.	Dal/seasonal vegetable	15	50 grams
3.	Edible oil	5	5 grams
4.	Masala	2	2 grams
5.	Onions	10	10 grams
6.	Salt	5	5 grams

Note: (1) 100 gram rice contains 340 calorie and 6.8 grams protein, (2) 15 gram dal contains 50 calorie and 2.9 grams protein, (3) 5 gram oil contains 45 calorie, and (4) 10 gram onion contains 5 calorie and 0.12 gram protein.

The following chart shows mechanism of supplying of foodgrains in the state.

Chart : Supply of Foodgrains

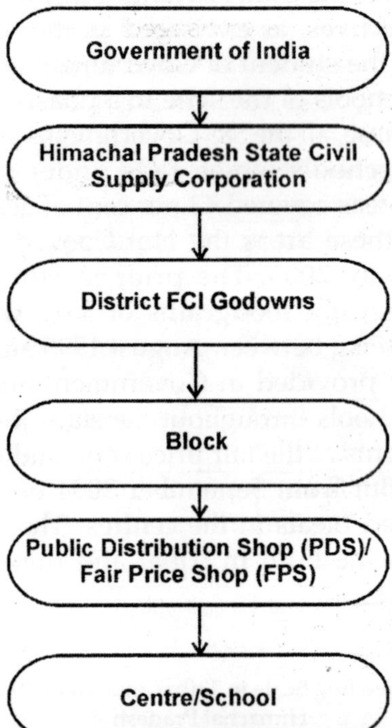

The teacher engaged in the scheme is bound to collect foodgrains from fair price shop and buy vegetables from the markets which affect the education of the children especially those schools where single teacher available. On the other side, required quantities of foodgrains are not provided to the schools but compensate the same in next stock by the local dealer.

Flow of Fund

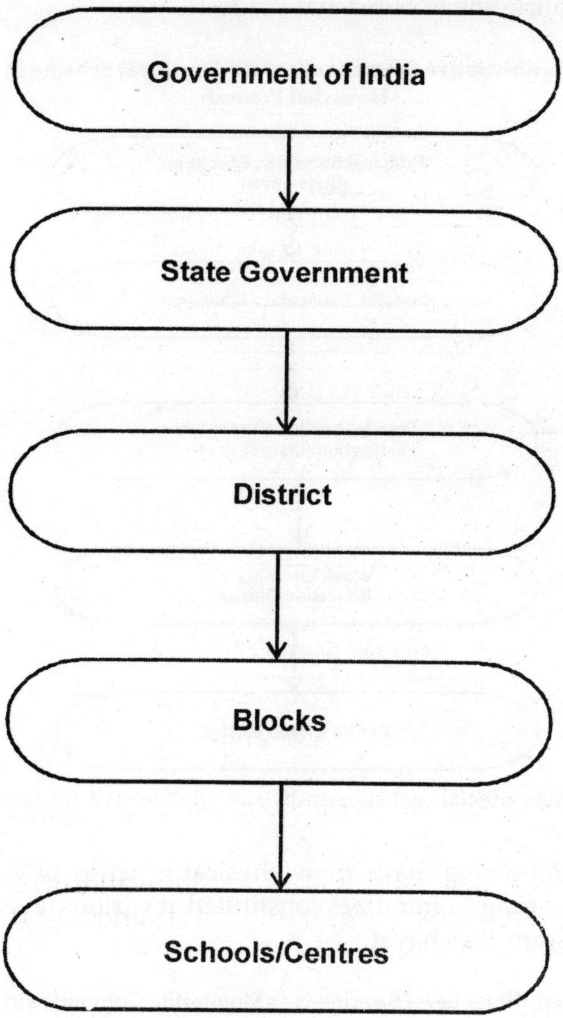
Government of India
State Government
District
Blocks
Schools/Centres

The following chart shows administrative set-up for Mid-day Meal Scheme in Himachal Pradesh.

Administrative Set-up for the Mid-Day Meal Scheme in Himachal Pradesh

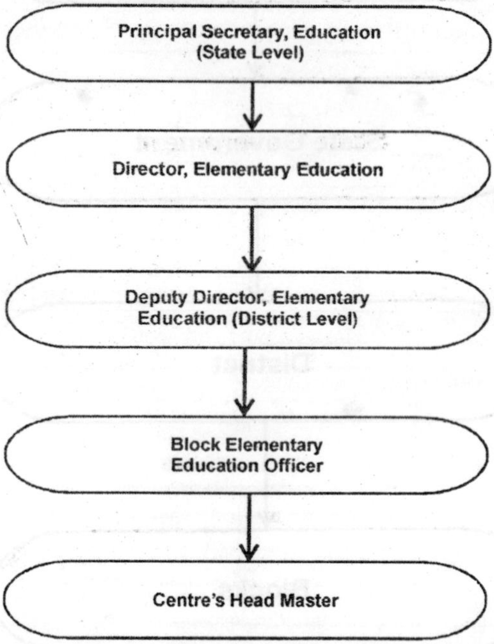

Note: All these officials get support by subordinate staff for running the scheme.

The following charts show physical structure of Steering-*cum*-Monitoring Committees constituted at various levels from State to Gram Panchayat.

Chart : State Level Steering-*cum*-Monitoring Committee in Himachal Pradesh

Sl. No.	*Designation of the Officer*	*Status*
1.	Chief Secretary	Chairman
2.	Principal Secretary, Education	Member
3.	Secretary, Rural Development	Member
4.	Secretary, Urban Development	Member
5.	Principal Secretary, Tribal Development	Member

(contd.)

Sl. No.	Designation of the Officer	Status
6.	Secretary, Health and Family Welfare	Member
7.	Principal Secretary, Food and Civil Supply	Member
8.	Secretary, Planning	Member
9.	Secretary, Social Justice and Empowerment	Member
10.	Secretary, Finance	Member
11.	Managing Director, HP State Civil Supplies Corporation	Member
12.	Senior, Regional Manager, Food Corporation of India (FCI)	Member
13.	2 Members of Parliament	Members
14.	4 Members of Legislative Assembly	Members
15.	Special Nutrition Officer, Department of Social Justice and Empowerment	Member
16.	2 Chairmen, Zilla Parishad	Members
17.	2 Retired Deputy Directors, Education	Members
18.	3 Deputy Commissioners	Members
19.	State President/General Secretary, HP Primary Teacher Federation	Member
20.	Director, Primary Education	Member-Secretary

This committee is formed in June 2005. The members of the committee are expected to meet at least once in 6 months. This committee furnishes information district-wise and ensures to supply of foodgrains to the schools enrolment-wise. The members of committee advocate menu area-wise and enhance financial support student-wise timely. The committee also creates basic facilities for smooth functioning of the scheme.

Chart : District Level Steering-*cum*-Monitoring Committee in Bilaspur

Sl. No.	Designation of the Officer	Status
1.	Deputy Commissioner	Chairman
2.	Chief Medical Officer	Member
3.	District Controller and Civil Supplies	Member
4.	Deputy Manager, FCI	Member
5.	President, Zilla Parishad	Member
6.	One representative, Municipal body	Member
7.	One expert from the area of Nutrition/Child Development	Member
8.	Four persons (2 women) who made significant contribution in the field of nutrition, child welfare, community mobilization	Members
9.	3-5 representatives of blocks/municipalities	Members
10.	One (At least) representatives of teacher	Member
11.	Deputy Director, Primary Education, HP	Member-Secretary

This committee expected to meet at least once in a month. The Deputy Director, Primary Education make allotment of foodgrains and allocation of funds according to enrolments of schools. The committee ensures proper distribution of Budget and make surprise visit randomly in at least 10 schools in each quarter and submit report to the Principal Secretary and Director of Primary Education.

Chart : Block Level Steering-*cum*-Monitoring Committee in Bilaspur

Sl. No.	*Designation of the Officer*	*Status*
1.	Sub-Divisional Officer, Civil	Chairman
2.	Block Medical Officer	Member
3.	Inspector, Food and Civil Supplies	Member
4.	Asstt. Manager/Depot In-charge, FCI	Member
5.	Block Development Officer	Member
6.	One expert from the area of Nutrition/Child Development	Member
7.	Four persons (2 women) with significant contribution in the field of nutrition/child welfare/community mobilization/school education/child health	Members
8.	3-5 representatives of Gram Panchayat	Members
9.	One (at least) representatives of teacher	Members
10.	Block Primary Education	Member-Secretary

The members of this committee are expected to meet at least once in a month. The Block Primary Education Officer recommends for allotment of foodgrains based on enrolments, centre-wise and make arrangement of distribution of foodgrains who also monitor and regulate actual delivery of foodgrains. The committee should ensure proper Budget distribution. The members can make surprise visit to the schools, etc.

Chart : Panchayat Level Steering-*cum*-Monitoring Committee in Himachal Pradesh

Sl. No.	*Designation of the Officer*	*Status*
1.	Pradhan (President) Gram Panchayat	President
2.	Head of the Centre (Head Master/Mistress)	Member-Secretary
3.	President, Mother Teacher Association (MTA)	Member
4.	Pradhan, Mahila Mandali/Shakti	Member

In Gumarwin I block, the President of Mahila Mandli/ Shakti are included in the Gram Panchayat Level Steering-*cum*-Monitoring Committee whereas in Gumarwin II block, first three members which shown in the above chart are involved in the Gram Panchayat Level Steering-*cum*-Monitoring Committee. The members of committee are expected to monitor the quantity and the quality of food serve at the centre, and make suitable suggestions timely for healthy and hygienic environment in the school premises.

Andhra Pradesh

The State Government of Andhra Pradesh has implemented various programmes like Back to School, Chaduvukundam, Chaduvula, etc. for promotion of Elementary Education in the state. Though much progress is achieved in enrolling school age children in the schools, the progress achieved in retention of all of them in the school is not commensurate with enrolment. One of the reasons identified is lack of nutritious food to the children which in turn has its impact on their educational development. To overcome this shortcoming, the Government has been implementing the National Programme for Nutritional Support to Primary Education (NSPE) by giving 3 kg of rice per month per child who puts 80 per cent of attendance. The Hon'ble Supreme Court of India in W.P.No.196/2001, dated 17.9.2001 directed that cooked meals should be provided to all primary school children in Government and Government assisted primary schools with a minimum content of 300 calories and 8-12 grams of protein each working day of the school. In the process of this, Government of Andhra Pradesh has decided to implement Mid-Day Meal Programme by giving hot cooked food in the school of Government (including local bodies) and aided primary and upper primary schools in the state from 2nd January, 2003 onwards with a minimum 300 calories, and 8-12 gram of protein content to each child on every school day. In Andhra Pradesh, this scheme has covered 70493 schools (in 2007) both Government and Government aided schools and provided benefit to 36 lakh boys and 25 lakh girls.

Cost per Child

Besides rice, the Government provides conversion cost to the per day per child in all the working days but not exceeding 220 days. The following chart shows cooking cost range-wise.

Chart : Range-wise convergence cost in Andhra Pradesh

Sl. No.	*Strength of the Children in the school*	*Unit Cost in Rs.*
1.	1-50	2.50
2.	51-100	2.25
3.	Above 100	2.00

Note: In the above range, the Government of India contributes Rs. 1.50 per day per child.

Weekly Menu in Andhra Pradesh

The Menu is flexible and the District Collector has got liberty to fix menu for the whole district or for various parts of the district for different days of the week. The following chart shows the weekly menu prescribed by the Government of Andhra Pradesh in all the three regions.

Chart : Weekly Menu in Andhra Pradesh

Sl. No.	*Day*	*Type of food supply*
1.	Monday	Rice, Sambher (Dal and Vegetable mixed)/Rasam
2.	Tuesday	Rice, Sambher
3.	Wednesday	Rice, Sambher
4.	Thursday	Rice, Sambher/Rasam
5.	Friday	Rice, Sambher
6.	Saturday	Rice, Sambher

In Andhra Pradesh, each student gets two eggs per week (Monday and Wednesday) with 120 gram rice everyday but those schools which covered by ISKCON and Kalahasti Temple Trust students get banana on the place of eggs.

Implementing Agency

In rural areas, women belonging to self-help groups, other agency like temple, Non-Governmental organizations of proven track record, charitable trusts/group of parents, (in order to preference) to be identified by the Mandal Revenue Officer, would be implementing agency. In urban areas, Community Development Societies/Non-Governmental organizations/Urban self-help groups/charitable trusts/group of parents (in order to preference) are identified by a committee headed by the Mandal Revenue Officer. In Andhra Pradesh, apart from the self-help groups, other agencies like Naandi Foundation, International Society for Krishna Consciousness (ISKCON) and Kalahasti Temple Trust are also running this scheme. Naandi Foundation covers 891 schools of the twin cities of Hyderabad and Secunderabad, and 111 schools of Visakhapatnam urban areas. The International Society for Krishna Consciousness (ISKCON) covers 33 and 32 schools both in urban and rural areas of Chittoor district nearby Tirupati. Similarly, the Kalahasti Temple Trust also covers 32 schools in rural areas of Chittoor district.

Committees for Monitoring and Supervision

The following chart shows the mechanism of monitoring and supervision of the scheme at various levels.

Chart : Steering-*cum*-Monitoring Committees at various levels in Andhra Pradesh

Sl. No.	*Name of the Committee*	*Members with Status*
1.	State level steering-*cum*-monitoring committee	Under Chairmanship of Chief Secretary
2.	District level steering-*cum*-monitoring committee	Under Chairmanship of District Collector
3.	Block level steering-*cum*-monitoring committee	Headed by Block Development Officer
4.	Panchayat level steering-*cum*-monitoring committee	Headed by President (Gram Panchayat)

These committees are expected to monitor function of the scheme, and also expected to make suitable suggestions. each committee comprising members of different backgrounds such as officials, experts of subject, social activists, leaders, members of the self-help group, etc. The following chart highlights the structure of each committee constituted from State to Gram Panchayat levels in Andhra Pradesh. All these committees monitor and supervise the functions of the scheme at various levels.

Chart : Composition of State Level Steering-*cum*-Monitoring Committee in Andhra Pradesh

Sl. No.	*Designation of the Officers*	*Status*
1.	Minister for School Education	Chairman
2.	Minister of Revenue	Member
3.	Minister of Panchayati Raj and Rural Development	Member
4.	Minister of Urban Development and Municipal Administration	Member
5.	Minister of Civil Supplies	Member
6.	Minister of Finance	Member
7.	Minister of Employment Generation	Member
8.	Secretary, Panchayati Raj	Member
9.	Secretary, Rural Department	Member
10.	Secretary, Tribal Development	Member
11.	Secretary, Social Welfare	Member
12.	Secretary, Urban Development and Municipality Administration	Member
13.	Secretary, Civil Supplies	Member
14.	Secretary, Finance	Member
15.	Commissioner and Director of School Education	Member
16.	Commissioner, Municipality of Hyderabad	Member
17.	State Project Director, District Primary Education Programme (DPEP)	Member
18.	Commissioner of Tribal Development	Member
19.	Commissioner of Social Welfare	Member
20.	Commissioner of BC Welfare	Member
21.	Commissioner of Women Empowerment	Member
22.	Director, Municipal Administration	Member
23.	State Project Director (SPD), Veluge	Member
24.	Secretary of School Education	Member-Secretary

Functions of State Level Steering-*cum*-Monitoring Com.nittee

1. This committee guiding various implementation agencies,
2. Monitor programme implementation, assessing its impact, and taking corrective steps,
3. Taking action on reports of independent monitoring/ education agencies,
4. Effective coordination and convergence among departments, agencies (e.g. FCI) and scheme,
5. Mobilizing community and promoting public private partnership for the programme,
6. This committee makes changes in menu timely and enhance amount to maintain quality of food so students would not get repeated food, and
7. This committee will meet at least once in every six months.

Chart : Composition of District Level Committee in Andhra Pradesh

Sl. No.	*Designation of the Officers*	*Status*
1.	District Collector	Chairman
2.	Joint Collector	Member
3.	Projector Director, District Rural Development Agency (DRDA)	Member
4.	Municipal Commissioner	Member
5.	Project Officer, Integrated Tribal Development Agency (ITDA)	Member
6.	District Supplies Officer	Member
7.	District Manager, Civil Supplies Corporation	Member
8.	Deputy Director, Social Welfare	Member
9.	District Tribal Welfare Officer	Member
10.	Backward Classes Welfare Officer	Member
11.	Additional Project Coordinator, DPEP	Member
12.	Project Director, Velugu Project	Member
13.	District Educational Officer	Member-Convener

Above committee meets once in a month and review performance of the scheme of whole district. The Joint Collector undertakes detailed planning, coordinates and furnishes monthly report to the Commissioner of the School Education on the implementation of mid-day meal in the district.

Chart : Composition of the Committee at Municipality Level in Andhra Pradesh

Sl. No.	Designation of the Officers	Status
1.	Joint Collector	Chairperson
2.	Municipal Commissioner	Member
3.	President of Children Development Society (CDS)	Member
4.	Two Head Masters	Member
5.	School Education Committee Chairpersons	Member
6.	Prominent NGOs/Corporate houses	Member
7.	District Education Officer	Member-Convener

There is a provision to constitute a separate committee at Municipality level which expected to review progress of the scheme in respective areas, and submits its monthly report to the concerned departments.

Chart : Composition of Committee at Mandal Level

Sl. No.	Designation of the Officers	Status
1.	Mandal Revenue Officer	Chairperson
2.	Mandal Parishad Development Officer	Member
3.	Mandal Resource Persons	Member
4.	Deputy Tahsildar, Civil Supplies Corporation of the areas	Member Member
5.	Mandal Education Officer	Member-Convener

This committee meets fortnightly and review performance of the scheme in whole Mandal.

Chart : Composition of Committee at Panchayat Level

Sl. No.	Designation of the Officers	Status
1.	Sarpanch, Gram Panchayat	Chairman
2.	Village Secretary	Member-Convener
3.	Mandal Parishad Teacher Committee	Member
4.	Chairpersons, School Education Committee in the Panchayat	Member
5.	President of DWCRA Group/SHGs implementing the programme	Member
6.	Head Masters of the Schools	Member
7.	Dealer, Fair Price Shop	Member

The general body of the gram panchayat review implementation of the scheme at village level and placed it in the gram sabha.

The following diagrams show mechanism of supply of foodgrains, flow of funds and administrative setup for implementation of the scheme in Andhra Pradesh.

Chart : Supply of Foodgrains

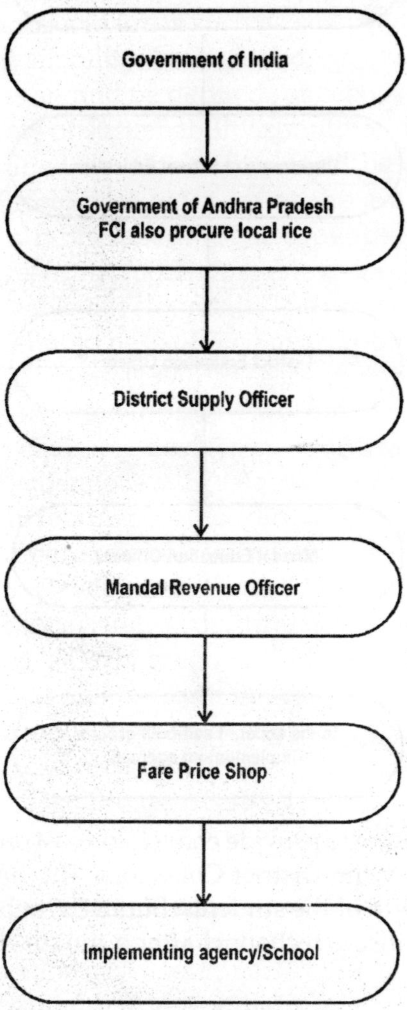

Chart : Flow of Fund

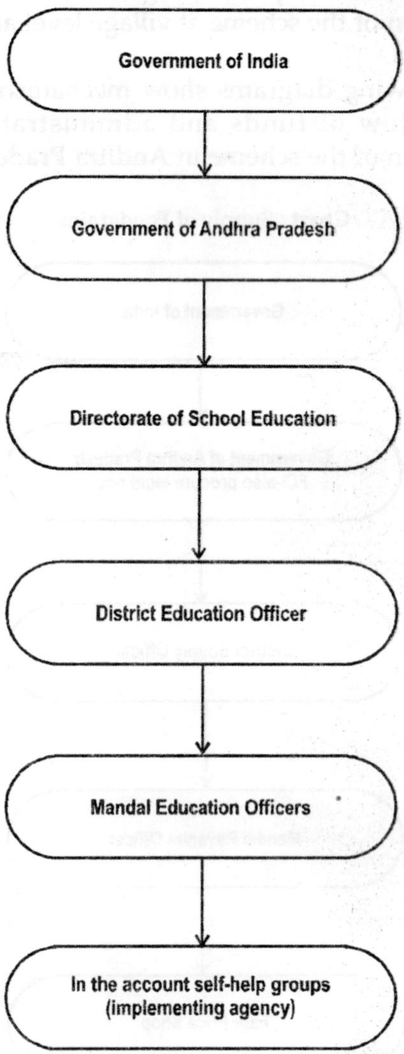

The provision to provide conversion cost on or before 20th of the month by the District Collectors. The fund is released based on strength of the students. Similarly, submission of the utilization certificate rechannel after a month from bottom to top.

Administrative set up for Implementation of the Scheme in Andhra Pradesh

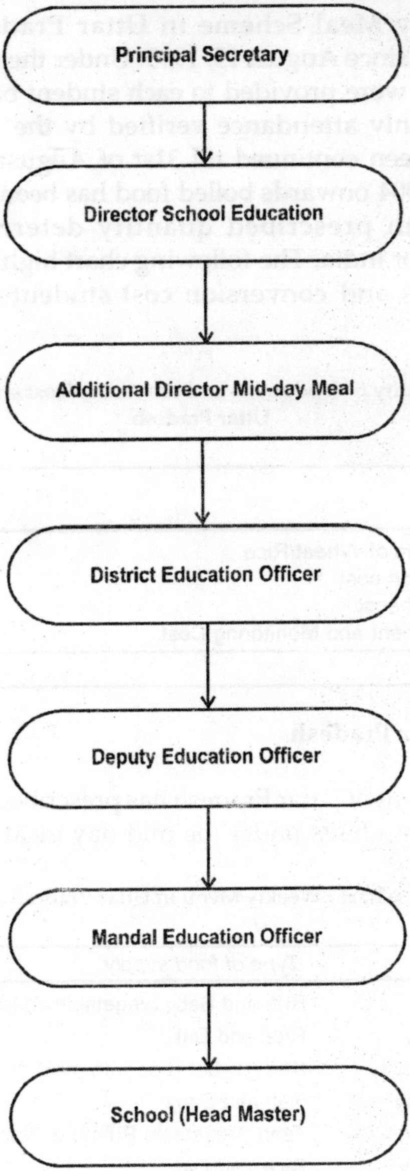

Uttar Pradesh

The Mid-Day Meal Scheme in Uttar Pradesh has been implemented since August 15, 1995. Under the scheme 3 kg of wheat or rice were provided to each student based on 80 per cent of monthly attendance verified by the teachers. This pattern has been continued till 31st of August, 2004 and 1st September, 2004 onwards boiled food has been serving to the students with prescribed quantity determined by the Government of India. The following chart highlights quantity of foodgrains and conversion cost student-wise in Uttar Pradesh.

Chart : Quantity of foodgrains and conversion cost student-wise in Uttar Pradesh

Sl. No.	*Items*	*Amount (Rs.)*
1.	100 grams of Wheat/Rice	1.11
2.	Conversion cost	2.00
3.	Transport cost	0.08
4.	Management and Monitoring Cost	0.02
	Total	3.31

Menu in Uttar Pradesh

The Government of Uttar Pradesh has prescribed the following menu for the students under the mid-day meal scheme.

Chart : Weekly Menu in Uttar Pradesh

Sl. No.	*Days*	*Type of food supply*
1.	Monday	Roti and Sabji (vegetables/curry)
2.	Tuesday	Rice and Dal
3.	Wednesday	Khir (Sweet Rice with milk) or Kadi-Rice
4.	Thursday	Roti and Sabji
5.	Friday	Tehri (Vegetable Pulao) or Namkin Daliya
6.	Saturday	Rice and Dal

Implementing Agency

The provision of supplying of cooked food in rural areas of Uttar Pradesh has been given to the Gram Panchayats. Similarly, in urban areas, ward and municipalities are responsible for supplying food to the students. Cook or helper collect foodgrains everyday from the Pradhan of the Gram Panchayats and prepare food in the school premises. The following chart shows composition of the different committees formed at various levels.

Chart : Composition of State Level Steering-*cum*-Monitoring Committee in Uttar Pradesh

Sl. No.	*Designation of the Officers*	*Status*
1.	Principal Secretary Education/Principal Secretary Basic Education	President
2.	Principal Secretary/Secretary Panchayati Raj	Member
3.	Principal Secretary/Secretary Employment	Member
4.	Principal Secretary/Secretary Finance	Member
5.	Principal Secretary/Secretary Urban Development	Member
6.	Principal Secretary/Secretary Food and Supply Department	Member
7.	Managing Director, Uttar Pradesh State Food and Essential Commodities	Member
8.	Director, Basic Education Department	Member Secretary
9.	Director, Panchayati Raj Department	Member
10.	Finance Controller, Uttar Pradesh Basic Education Council	Member

This Committee reviews and monitors function of the scheme, and make change for better function of the scheme in whole state.

Chart : Composition of District Level Steering-*cum*-Monitoring Committee in Uttar Pradesh

Sl. No.	Designation of the Officers	Status
1.	District Collector	President
2.	Chief Development Officer	Member
3.	District Education Inspector	Member-Secretary
4.	District Programme Officer	Member
5.	District Supply Officer	Member
6.	Chief Medical Officer	Member
7.	Deputy Chief Medical Officers	Member
8.	District Development Officer	Member
9.	Project Director DRDA	Member
10.	District Social Welfare Officer	Member
11.	District Panchayati Raj Officer	Member
12.	District Basic Officer	Member
13.	Commissioner/Executive Officer Municipality	Member
14.	District Officer Food and Essential Commodities	Member

This Committee meets once in a month, and reviews progress of the scheme in the district.

Chart : Composition of Block Level Steering-*cum*-Monitoring Committee in Uttar Pradesh

Sl. No.	Designation of the Officers	Status
1.	Sub-Divisional Magistrate	Chairman
2.	Assistant Basic Education Officer	Member-Convener
3.	Block Development Officer	Member
4.	Medical Officer at Block Level	Member
5.	Deputy Block Development Officer, Panchayat	Member
6.	Deputy Tahsildar	Member
7.	Officer (one) nominated by Deputy Collector	Member
8.	Supply Inspector	Member

The members of the committee assemble once in a month and review the progress of the scheme.

Chart : Composition of Gram Panchayat Level Steering-*cum*-Monitoring Committee in Uttar Pradesh

Sl. No.	Designation of the Officers	Status
1.	Gram Pradhan/Sarpanch	President
2.	Two Women (guardians) nominated by Gram Pradhan	Members
3.	Head Master/Head Mistress	Member-Convener
4.	Two Men (guardians) nominated by Gram Pradhan	Members

The Pradhan of Gram Panchayat make arrangement of providing cooked food to the students whereas in urban areas ward members assigned to make arrangement of cooked food to the students. In urban areas, a similar type of committee constituted at municipality level which monitor the scheme.

The following diagrams show mechanism of supplying of foodgrains, flow of funds and administrative setup for implementation of the scheme in Uttar Pradesh.

Chart : Supply of Foodgrains

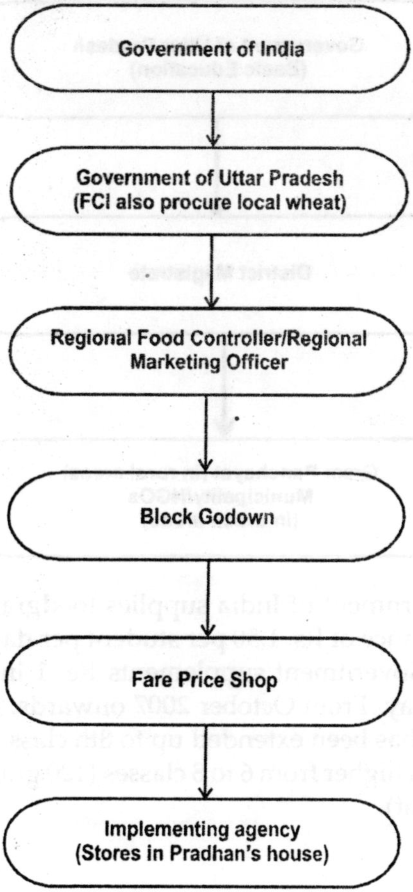

The guidelines of the scheme indicate that the foodgrains should be kept in the school premises but Pradhans, in general, keep foodgrains in their house because of threat of thief.

Chart : Flow of Fund

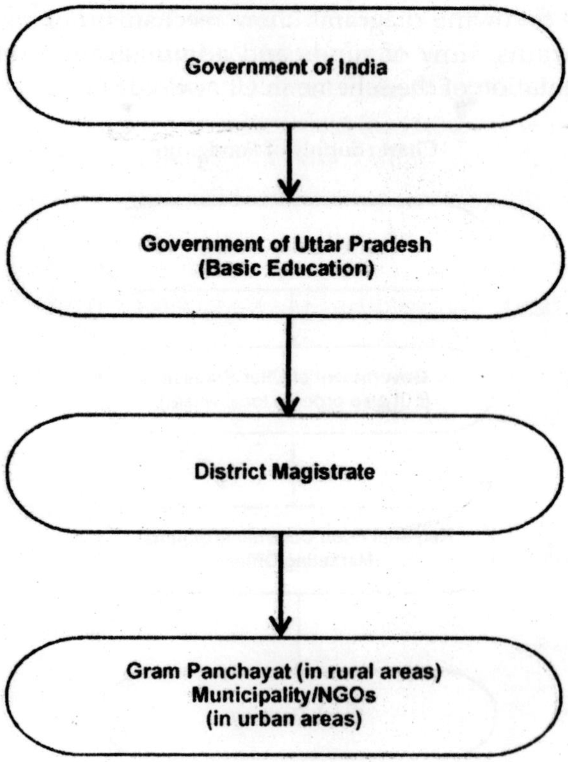

The Government of India supplies foodgrains including financial assistance of Rs. 1.50 per student per day. In addition to this, State Government supplements Re. 1 in case of each student each day. From October 2007 onwards, the facility of mid-day meal has been extended up to 8th class. The quantity of foodgrains is higher from 6 to 8 classes (120 gram foodgrains for each student).

Administrative set up for Implementation of the Scheme in Uttar Pradesh

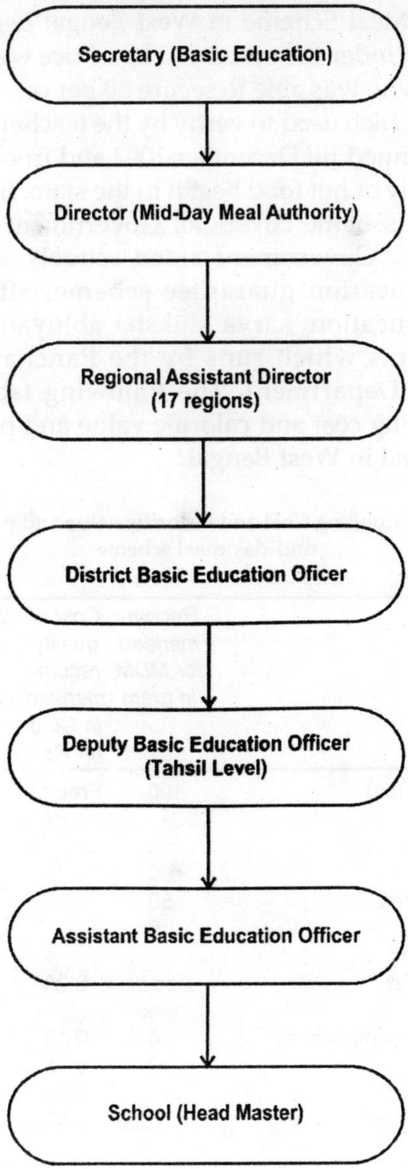

West Bengal

The Mid-day Meal Scheme in West Bengal began from 15th August, 1995. Under the scheme, 3 kg of rice were supplied to each student who was able to secure 80 per cent of attendance monthly and which used to verify by the teachers. This pattern has been continued till December 2002 and from January 2003 onwards supply of hot food began in the state. In West Bengal, mid-day meal scheme covers all Government schools, local bodies schools, Government aided schools, schools under centres of education guarantee scheme, alternative and innovative education, sarva shiksha abhiyan, madhyamik shiksha kendras which runs by the Panchayats of Rural Development Department. The following table highlights norms of cooking cost and calorific value and protein content of mid-day meal in West Bengal.

Chart : Norms of Cooking Cost and Calorific value and protein content of mid-day meal scheme

Sl. No.	*Items*	*Recommended for MDM in gram*	*Cost of quality recommended in CL.3 (in Rs.)*	*Energy content (in calories)*	*Protein content (in grams)*
1	Foodgrains (rice)	100	Free of cost	340	8
2	Cooking Cost				
	(i) Pulse	30	0.75	105	7
	(ii) Vegetables	60	0.60	30	0
	(a) Leafy	5			
	(b) Others				
	(iii) Oil and fat	As per need	0.25	45	0
	(iv) Salt and condiments	0	0.15	0	0
	(v) Fuel	0	0.15	0	0
	(vi) Labour and		0.25	0	0
	(vii) Other administrative charges		0.50	0	0
		2.50	**520**	**15**	

Menu in West Bengal

The Government of West Bengal has prescribed the following menu for the students under the mid-day meal scheme.

Chart : Weekly Menu in West Bengal

S.No.	*Days*	*Type of food supply*
1.	Monday	Rice, Dal and Vegetable
2.	Tuesday	Rice, Dal and Vegetable
3.	Wednesday	Rice, Dal and Soyabean, egg
4.	Thursday	Rice, Dal and Vegetable
5.	Friday	Rice, Dal and Vegetable, egg
6.	Saturday	Rice, Dal and Vegetable

The above menu is decided by State Level Steering-*cum*-Monitoring Committee but flexibility has been given to the district and block level committees to change above menu according to local food habit.

Implementing Agency

The provision of supplying of cooked food in rural areas of West Bengal is given to the local self-help groups. The involved members get Rs. 600 per month and which equally share by them. In urban areas, (at municipality level), the same mechanism has been adopted. In Kolkata proper, a non-Governmental Organization, namely City Level Programme of Action for Street and Working Children involves in running of the scheme with the association of other 64 alien non-Governmental Organizations, which cover 141 wards of the city.

Chart : Composition of State Level Steering-*cum*-Monitoring Committee in West Bengal

Sl. No.	*Designation of the Officers*	*Status*
1.	Chief Secretary, Government of West Bengal	President
2.	Principal Secretary, School Education Department	Member-Secretary
3.	Principal Secretary, Development and Planning Department	Member
4.	Principal Secretary, Panchayati Raj and Rural Development	Member
5.	Commissioner of School Education	Member
6.	Karmadhyaksha Shipshape Sthayee Samity	Member
7.	President, West Bengal Board of Primary Education	Member
8.	President, West Bengal Board of Madrasah Education	Member
9.	President, West Bengal Board of Secondary Education	Member
10.	Nominated persons of different fields	Members

In West Bengal, no separate body has been constituted for monitoring of the scheme at State Level but the issues related to mid-day meal scheme are discussed under the State Level Committee of Sarva Shiksha Abhiyan (SSA).

Chart : Composition of District Level Steering-*cum*-Monitoring Committee, West Bengal

Sl.No.	*Designation of the Officers*	*Status*
1.	District Collector	President
2.	Member of Legislative Assembly (2)	Members
3.	Assistant District Magistrate	Member-Secretary
4.	District Inspector of Schools	Member
5	District Controller (Food and Supply)	Member
6.	District Manager of FCI	Member
7.	Chief Medical Officer	Member
8.	Representatives of Municipality	Member
9.	MARE	Member
10.	Chairman of District Primary Council	Member
11.	District Karmadhikari	Member

This Committee meets once in a month to review the progress of the scheme.

Chart : Composition of Block Level Steering-*cum*-Monitoring Committee in West Bengal

Sl. No.	*Designation of the Officers*	*Status*
1.	Sub-Divisional Officer	President
2.	Block Development Officer	Member-Secretary
3.	Inspector of Schools	Member
4.	Elected Representatives of Pachyayat Samitis	Members

The above committee review performance of the scheme once in a month and advise suitable suggestions. At village level, no separate committee has been constituted for the scheme but monitoring of the scheme has been handed over to Village Education Committee (VEC) which headed by the President/Sarpach supported by other representatives of mother teacher association and parent teacher association.

The following diagrams show mechanism of supplying of foodgrains, flow of funds and administrative set-up for implementation of the scheme in West Bengal.

Chart : Supply of Foodgrains

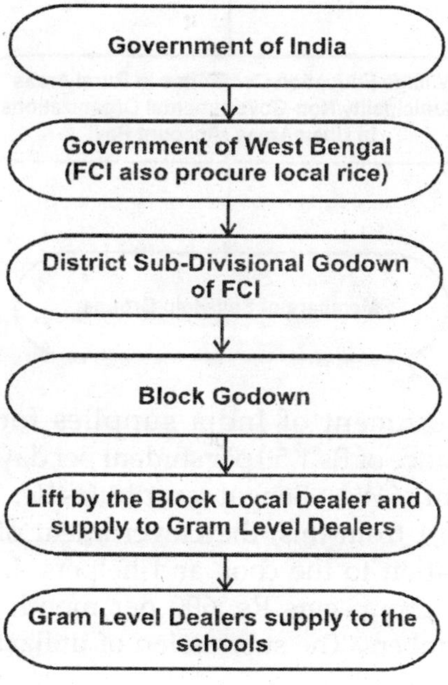

Chart : Flow of Fund

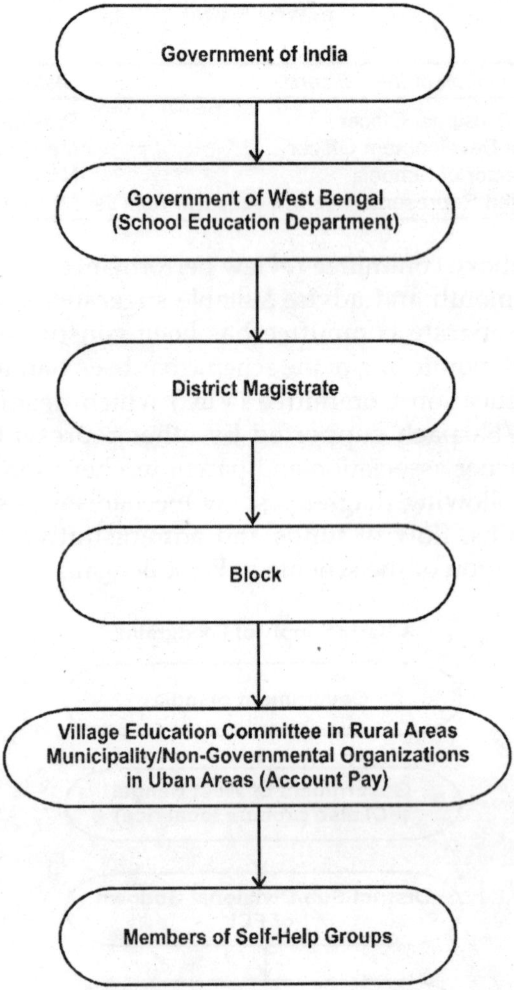

The Government of India supplies foodgrains and financial assistance of Rs.1.50 per student per day and on which the Government of West Bengal contributes Re. 1 student-wise everyday. Apart from this, the Government of West Bengal pays remuneration to the cook and helpers. In this process, each self-help group gets Rs. 600 per month which shares among the members. The submission of utilization certificate both for consumption of foodgrains and allotted funds furnish from bottom to top means from school to block, block to district, district to state, and from state to centre which is similar in case of all the studied states.

Administrative set up for Implementation of the Scheme in West Bengal

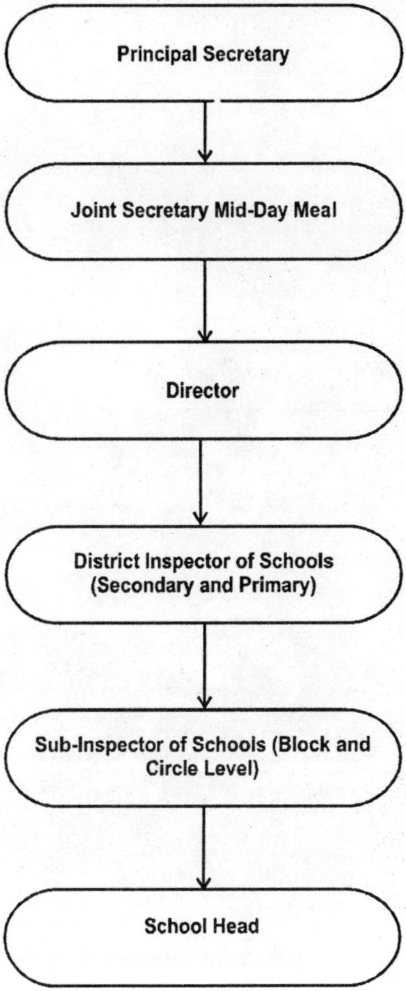

Photographs

Tamil Nadu : Students having food

Tamil Nadu : Students having food

Gujarat : Women preparing food

Gujarat : Officials with cooking staff (A view of kitsch shed)

Himachal Pradesh : Women cooking food

Himachal Pradesh : Students having food

Andhra Pradesh : Students collecting food

Andhra Pradesh : SHG members and weight machine

Uttar Pradesh : Women preparing Chapatti

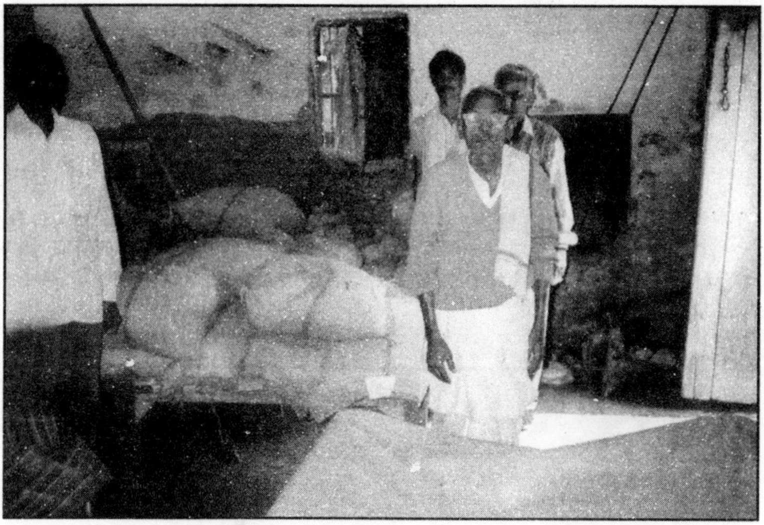

Uttar Pradesh : Pradhan stores foodgrains at home

West Bengal : SHG members cooking

West Bengal : SHG members serving food

3

Infrastructure in Schools

Infrastructure plays a significant role to tie up students with education. Infrastructure creates curiosity for development of education especially students belonging to the weaker sections who show low interest towards education due to various reasons as stated in last chapter. This study paid attention to find out availability of infrastructure and basic facilities in sample schools in the form of electricity, sources of drinking water, kitchen shed, utensils for cooking, availability of toilet both for students and teachers, student-teacher ratio, approach road, etc.

The following table shows the availability of link road and radius of link road in all the sample schools.

Table 3.1: Availability of link road in sample schools of Tamil Nadu, Gujarat and Himachal Pradesh

Sl. No.	*State*	*Availability of link road*		*Total*
		Yes	*No*	
1.	Tamil Nadu	17	3	20
2.	Gujarat	18	2	20
3.	Himachal Pradesh	12	8	20
	Total	**47 (78.3%)**	**13 (21.7%)**	**60 (100.0%)**

The above-mentioned table shows that 78.3 per cent (47) schools in all the three states were connected with the *pucca* roads whereas 21.7 per cent (13) schools were not connected with the *pucca* roads. In Himachal Pradesh, a sizable number, i.e. 8 (40.0 per cent) of the schools were not connected with the *pucca* roads because of hilly terrain. In Gujarat, 2 (10 per cent) schools were not having accessibility with the *pucca* road which was falling in the tribal dominated block. In general, *pucca* or semi-roads motivate students to touch schools regularly even in rainy season too.

The following table shows availability of electricity in sample schools in all the three states.

Table 3.2: Availability of electricity in sample schools of Tamil Nadu, Gujarat and Himachal Pradesh

Sl. No.	State	Availability of Electricity		Total
		Yes	No	
1.	Tamil Nadu	20	—	20
2.	Gujarat	19	1	20
3.	Himachal Pradesh	15	5	20
	Total	**54 (90.0%)**	**6 (10.0%)**	**60 (100.0%)**

The above table shows that 90.0 per cent (54) sample schools in all the three states were electrified whereas 10.0 per cent (6) schools were not having electricity in the premises. In Himachal Pradesh this number was high than other two states. All the 5 schools in Himachal Pradesh were located far than the main hamlets where the facility of electricity was not provided.

The following table shows availability of safe drinking water in school premises.

Table 3.3: Availability of safe drinking water in sample schools of Tamil Nadu, Gujarat and Himachal Pradesh

Sl. No.	State	Whether the potable drinking water available in school premises		Total
		Yes	No	
1.	Tamil Nadu	20	—	20
2.	Gujarat	20	—	20
3.	Himachal Pradesh	20	—	20
	Total	**60 100.0%**	**—**	**60 100.0%**

The above-mentioned table shows availability of sources of drinking water in the sample schools of three states. All sample schools in three states have got the facility of drinking water. In Tamil Nadu and Himachal Pradesh, almost all the schools were connected with the tap water whereas in Gujarat sample schools were connected with the hand pumps. A few sample schools of Tamil Nadu and in Himachal Pradesh were accessible for both, i.e. tap as well hand pumps.

Table 3.4: Availability of lavatory in sample schools of Tamil Nadu, Gujarat and Himachal Pradesh

Sl. No.	*State*	*Availability of Lavatory*		*Total*
		Yes	*No*	
1.	Tamil Nadu	20	—	20
2.	Gujarat	20	—	20
3.	Himachal Pradesh	20	—	20
	Total	**60** **100.0%**	**—**	**60** **100.0%**

The above-mentioned table shows that all sample schools in three states were having the facility of lavatories either in one or other form. It is noticed that no common criteria have been adopted in this regard. In all the sample schools, either one common lavatory has been provided between the female teachers and the girls or separate lavatory has been provided for the female teachers and the girls. But in case of boys, it is observed that they were not allowed to use such lavatories which meant for the male teachers. It is further noticed that wherever the numerical strength of students were high there separate lavatories were provided for boys, girls and for the staff both male and female teachers.

The following table shows the availability of rooms in all sample schools in three states.

Table 3.5: Availability of number of rooms in sample schools of Tamil Nadu, Gujarat and Himachal Pradesh

Sl. No.	*States*	*Number of rooms in schools*					*Total*
		2 Rooms	*4 Rooms*	*5 Rooms*	*6 Rooms*	*13 Rooms*	
1.	Tamil Nadu	3	5	4	7	1	20
2.	Gujarat	3	9	5	3	—	20
3.	Himachal Pradesh	8	5	5	2	—	20
	Total	**14** **23.3%**	**19** **31.7%**	**14** **23.3%**	**12** **20.0%**	**1** **1.67%**	**60** **100.0%**

The above-mentioned table shows that in Tamil Nadu, one school has got 13 rooms whereas majority of the schools have got rooms between the ranges of 2-6. The situation was noticed in case of sample schools of Gujarat and Himachal Pradesh. In Tamil Nadu, foodgrains store in kitchen shed whereas in Gujarat and Himachal Pradesh foodgrains keep in one of the rooms which also uses simultaneously for teaching purpose. In Himachal Pradesh, due to shortage of rooms food is being cooked in the same room where students sit which may lead to hazard as many of the schools (19 out of 20 sample schools) in Himachal Pradesh have got connection of LPG. As far as rooms are concerned, it is noticed that no common policy has been adopted even students are numerically high or low compared to one or other school.

The following table shows availability of the kitchen shed in sample schools of three states.

Table 3.6: Availability of kitchen sheds in sample schools of Tamil Nadu, Gujarat and Himachal Pradesh

Sl. No.	*State*	*Whether Kitchen Shed is available*		*Total*
		Yes	*No*	
1.	Tamil Nadu	19	1	20
2.	Gujarat	13	7	20
3.	Himachal Pradesh	4	16	20
	Total	**36** **(60.0%)**	**24** **(40.0%)**	**60** **(100.0%)**

The above table shows that in Tamil Nadu majority of the schools have got facility of kitchen shed whereas in Gujarat 65.0 per cent (13) of the schools and in Himachal Pradesh 20.0 per cent (4) of the schools have got facility of kitchen shed. The availability of kitchen shed in most of the schools in Tamil Nadu indicates that this scheme in Tamil Nadu is well organized and in matured stage and it has become a part of the educational system. In Gujarat, kitchen sheds were constructed under the funds of Tribal Sub-Plan, and Swarnjayanit Gramin Rojgar Yojana (SGRY). In Himachal Pradesh, kitchen sheds were constructed under the funds of District Institute of Education and Training (DIET). Government of India has now made allocation of Rs. 60,000 for construction of kitchen shed.

The following table shows figures of Andhra Pradesh, Uttar Pradesh and West Bengal where samples of the schools have been drawn 60 in each state. The below mentioned table shows a comparative picture of Andhra Pradesh, Uttar Pradesh and West Bengal of availability of link road with the schools.

Table 3.7: Availability of link road in sample schools of Andhra Pradesh, Uttar Pradesh and West Bengal

Sl. No.	*State*	*Availability of link road*		*Total*
		Yes	No	
1.	Andhra Pradesh	57 95.0%	3 0.5%	60 100.0%
2.	Uttar Pradesh	58 96.6	2 3.4	60 100.0%
3.	West Bengal	57 95.0%	3 0.5%	60 100.0%
	Total	**172 (95.5%)**	**08 (4.45%)**	**180 (100.0%)**

The above-mentioned table shows that 95.5 per cent (57) of the schools in Andhra Pradesh, and similarly in West Bengal were connected with the *pucca* roads whereas in Uttar Pradesh 96.6 per cent (58) schools were connected with the *pucca* roads. It is observed that those schools which were not connected with the *pucca* roads immediately were having the facility of *pucca* roads within the range of 1 or 2 km.

The following table shows availability of electricity in sample schools of all the three states.

Table 3.8: Availability of electricity in sample schools of Andhra Pradesh, Uttar Pradesh and West Bengal

Sl. No.	*States*	*Availability of basic facility—electricity*		*Total*
		Yes	*No*	
1.	Andhra Pradesh	20 33.3%	40 66.7%	60 100.0%
2.	Uttar Pradesh	19 31.7%	41 68.3%	60 100.0%
3.	West Bengal	33 55.0%	27 45.0%	60 100.0%
	Total	**72 (40.0%)**	**108 (60.0%)**	**180 (100.0%)**

The above table shows that 40.0 per cent (72) of the schools in all the three states were having connection of electricity whereas 60.0 per cent (108) schools were not having electricity in the school premises. In this proportionate Andhra Pradesh is lagging behind than other two states. It is noticed that a large number of sample schools in Telengana region of Andhra Pradesh had tide illegal connection with nearby electricity poles.

The following table shows availability of safe drinking water in school premises.

Table 3.9: Availability of safe drinking water in sample schools of Andhra Pradesh, Uttar Pradesh and West Bengal

Sl. No.	*State*	*Weather the potable drinking water available in school premises*		*Total*
		Yes	*No*	
1.	Andhra Pradesh	60 100.0%	— —	60 100.0%
2.	Uttar Pradesh	60 100.0%	— —	60 100.0%
3.	West Bengal	59 98.3%	1 1.7%	60 100.0%
	Total	**179 (99.4%)**	**1 (0.6%)**	**180 (100.0%)**

The above table shows that most of the schools in all the three states do have facility of safe drinking water in school premises except one school which located in sample areas of West Bengal.

Table 3.10: Types of sources available for drinking water in sample schools of Andhra Pradesh, Uttar Pradesh and West Bengal

Sl. No.	*State*	*Type of potable drinking water*			*Total*
		Tap	*Hand pump*	*Both*	
1.	Andhra Pradesh	53 83.3%	6 10.0%	1 1.7%	60 100.0%
2.	Uttar Pradesh	—	60 100.0%	—	60 100.0%
3.	West Bengal	—	60 100.0%	—	60 100.0%
	Total	**53 (29.4%)**	**126 (70.0%)**	**1 (0.6%)**	**180 (100.0%)**

The above-mentioned table shows that 70.0 per cent (126) of the schools were connected with hand pumps whereas 29.4 per cent (53) of the schools were having facility of the tap water. It is noticed that hand pumps are the major sources of supplying of drinking water to the children especially in Uttar Pradesh and West Bengal. In sample schools of Andhra Pradesh, majority of the schools were connected with the tap water which as precautionary measure especially in case of Telengana where fluoride contamination is higher than the rest of the state. The sample district (Nalgonda) has acute problem in this regard.

The following table shows that 48.3 per cent (29) in Andhra Pradesh have got the facility of lavatory in school premises for teachers. 31.1 (56) per cent schools of three states were lacking of separate toilet facility in which schools coming under the preview of Uttar Pradesh and West Bengal were high. 11.1 (20) per cent schools were having common toilet for girls and female teachers. A sizable number, i.e. 41.1 per cent (74) schools in all the three states were not having toilet. In case of few schools lock being used to avoid accessibility for the boys. It is noticed that maintenance of toilets was poor in most of the schools.

Table 3.11: Availability of lavatory in sample schools of Andhra Pradesh, Uttar Pradesh and West Bengal

Sl. No.	State	Availability of Lavatory/Toilet					Total
		Staff	Girls	No separate toilet	No Toilet	Staff and Girls	
1.	Andhra Pradesh	29 48.3%	1 1.7%	13 21.7%	17 28.3%	—	60 100.0%
2.	Uttar Pradesh	—	—	1 1.7%	39 65.0%	20 33.3%	60 100.0%
3.	West Bengal	—	—	42 70.0%	18 30.0%	—	60 100.0%
	Total	29 **(16.1%)**	1 **(0.6%)**	56 **(31.1%)**	74 **(41.1%)**	20 **(11.1%)**	180 **(100.0%)**

Table 3.12 shows the availability of rooms in all sample schools in three states.

The following table shows in Andhra Pradesh one-fourth (15) of schools got two rooms whereas in Uttar Pradesh 8.3 per cent (5) schools were having facility of two rooms. In West Bengal, 30.0 per cent (18) schools have got four rooms. Similarly in West Bengal itself one school has got 10 rooms. This study finds 20.0 per cent (36) schools in all the three states have got five rooms. In case of rooms, no uniformity has been maintained even wherever students numerically were high shortage of rooms noticed and wherever students were less more rooms were found.

Table 3.12: Availability of rooms in sample schools of Andhra Pradesh, Uttar Pradesh and West Bengal

Sl. No.	*State*	*Number of rooms in schools*										*Total*
		1 Rooms	*2 Rooms*	*3 Rooms*	*4 Rooms*	*5 Rooms*	*6 Rooms*	*7 Rooms*	*8 Rooms*	*9 Rooms*	*10 Rooms*	
1.	Andhra Pradesh	9	15	14	1	12	5	3	1	—	—	**60**
		15.0%	25.0%	23.3%	1.7%	20.0%	8.3%	5.0%	1.7%			**100.0%**
2.	Uttar Pradesh	—	5	9	21	15	5	4	—	1	—	**60**
			8.3%	15.0%	35.0%	25.0%	8.3%	6.7%		1.7%		**100.0%**
3.	West Bengal	5	—	6	18	9	13	4	2	2	1	**60**
		8.3%		10.0%	30.0%	15.0%	21.7%	6.7%	3.3%	3.3%	1.7%	**100.0%**
	Total	14	20	29	40	36	23	11	3	3	1	180
		7.8%	11.1%	16.1%	22.2%	20.0%	12.8%	6.1%	1.7%	1.7%	0.6%	100.0%

The following table shows the availability of kitchen shed in sample schools in three states.

Table 3.13: Availability of kitchen shed in sample schools of Andhra Pradesh, Uttar Pradesh and West Bengal

Sl. No.	*State*	*Whether Kitchen Shed is available?*		*Total*
		Yes	*No*	
1.	Andhra Pradesh	42 70.0%	18 30.0%	60 100.0%
2.	Uttar Pradesh	50 83.4%	10 16.6%	60 100.0%
3.	West Bengal	40 66.7%	20 33.3%	60 100.0%
	Total	**132** (73.33%)	**48** (26.67%)	**180** (100.0%)

The above table shows that majority of 73.33 per cent (132) schools in the three states were having facility of the kitchen sheds whereas 26.67 per cent (48) schools were lacking such facility. In Andhra Pradesh and in Uttar Pradesh majority of the schools were having kitchen sheds whereas in West Bengal kitchen sheds were of tinsheds. It is noticed that all the sample schools (20) in Malda district were lacking facility of kitchen sheds. The kitchen sheds have been constructed under various schemes like Sampoorna Gramin Rozgar Yojana (SGRY), Pachayats funds, Untied funds, District Institute of Education and Training (DPEP), 10th Finance teacher's contribution, Jawahar Rozgar Yojana (JRY), Sarva Shiksha Abhiyan (SSA), etc. in all the three states.

The student-teacher ratio has not found uniform as per requirements like 1:40, which differs from school to school even in the same block despite numerical strength of the students are almost similar in nature. To sort out shortage of teachers, the provision has been made to employee Vidhya Volunteers on consolidated remuneration of Rs. 1,500 per month under Sarva Shiksha Abhiyan. Under this system local persons both male and female get employment. Their remunerations are being paid from the funds of Sarva Shiksha Abhiyan. But it is noticed that Vidhya Volunteers were not getting remunerations in time.

4

Coverage of the Scheme

In rural areas, education point of view, children are still behind due to various reasons such as poverty, migration of the parents, economic constraint of the family, lack of environment, due to low aptitude towards the need of education, prevalent of child labour due to mitigate basic requirements of day-to-day or otherwise children use as mode of incomes, lack of basic infrastructure in schools, lack of teachers, apathetic attitude of the teachers, social bias, no immediate return from the education in terms of maintaining livelihood or due to low priorities of education, domestic work or otherwise taking care of siblings especially when parents go out for work, etc. are some of the causes which lead low enrolment. To resolve these problems, mid-day meal scheme is one of the illuminative processes. This scheme promotes enrolment of the students and maintains enrolment constantly high. This scheme gives relief to the poor parents who are not able to take care of their children due to poverty and children get food at the shake of educational development. This scheme attracts students to attend school regularly. To understand the impact of the scheme, this study covers enrolment, retention, drop-out and results of the students from last five years i.e. 2001-02 to 2006-07 which have been placed in next chapter.

The following table shows comparative picture of all the six states in case of number of total schools in each state, number of schools where the scheme has been implementing, number of beneficiaries (students) availing the facility of mid-day meal in 2006-07.

Table 4.1: State-wise scenario of the scheme (in December 2006)

Sl. No.	*State*	*No. of total schools primary and middle*	*No. of schools where scheme implementing*	*No. of students availed benefit (in lakhs)*
1.	Tamil Nadu	41344	41344	61.94
2.	Gujarat	31682	29991	48.78
3.	Himachal Pradesh	10975	10839	5.77
	Total	**84001**	**82174**	**116.49**

Table 4.2: State-wise scenario of the scheme (in December 2007)

Sl. No.	*State*	*No. of total schools primary level*	*No. of schools where scheme implemented*	*No. of students availed benefit (in lakhs)*
1.	Andhra Pradesh	136500	136500	50.73
2.	Uttar Pradesh	93973	93973	18.41
3.	West Bengal	76310	71321	93.46
	Total	**306783**	**301794**	**162.60**

Both the above-mentioned tables show that students of primary schools in Himachal Pradesh and Uttar Pradesh are less comparatively other states in utilization of benefit of the scheme even though Uttar Pradesh has got high population. The higher beneficiaries recorded in West Bengal followed by Tamil Nadu, Andhra Pradesh, and Gujarat.

The following table shows district-wise scenario of the scheme in term of schools, number of schools covered and students availed the facility of mid-day meal scheme.

Table 4.3: District-wise scenario of the scheme in different states (December 2006)

Sl. No.	*District*	*Total schools*	*Total centre/ schools covered*	*Total students covered under scheme*			*Total*
				Primary	*Upper Primary*	*Primary Middle*	
1	Kanchipuram (TN)	1242	1242	125210 64.9%	—	67755 35.1%	192965 (100.0%)
2	Sabarkanta (Gujarat)	2507	2486	161010 79.9%	40307 20.1%	—	201317 (100.0%)
3	Bilaspur (HP)	591	591	26994 100.0%	—	—	26994 (100.0%)
	Total	**4340**	**4319**	**313214 (74.3%)**	**40307 (9.6%)**	**677.5 (16.1%)**	**421236 (100.0%)**

The above table shows in Kanchipuram district of Tamil Nadu 64.9 per cent students covered under primary level whereas in 35.1 per cent of students covered under middle standard. Similarly, in Sabarkanta district of Gujarat 79.9 per cent students got hot food up to primary level whereas 20.1 per cent of students covered up to upper primary level. In both states, beyond primary level the expenditure is borne by the State Government. In Himachal Pradesh, the facility of mid-day meal provides up to the primary level students. In Tamil Nadu out of 1242 schools, this scheme has been implementing in 986 primary schools and 256 middle schools which exist between VI to VIII classes. In Gujarat, the benefit of the scheme has been provided up to VII standard which comes under the category of upper primary. In Himachal Pradesh, this scheme has been facilitated up to the primary schools which cover Classes I-V. In Tamil Nadu and Gujarat, beyond primary, the expenditure of the scheme has been borne by the concerned states, but now the benefit of the scheme has been extended up to upper primary level. Presently the Government of Tamil Nadu has extended the benefit of the scheme up to the 10th standard with their own state cost whereas rest of states provides benefit of the scheme up to upper primary with the assistance of Government of India.

The following table shows coverage of the student in primary schools region-wise in all the three states. In all states, Government of India supply foodgrains up to the primary level for 220 days along with convergence cost of Rs.1.50 per student per school day. Apart from this concerned State Government add financial assistance to run the scheme. The Government of Andhra Pradesh contributes 1.00 rupee, 75 paisa and 0.50 paisa simultaneously for the strength of up to 50, between 51 and 100, and above 101 per student per day whereas Government of Uttar Pradesh contributes 0.50 paisa per student per day, and Government of West Bengal bears rupee 1.0 per student per day to boost scheme up to primary level.

Table 4.4: District-wise status of the scheme (December 2007)

Sl. No.	*Selected Districts in the different region*	*Total Primary Schools*	*Total Students covered*
1.	Nalgonda	2614	174856
2.	Guntur	2870	196837
3.	Chittoor	4183	178774
4.	Lakhimpur Kheri	2250	466394
5.	Allahabad	2225	514517
6.	Jhansi	997	169230
7.	North 24 Parganas	5075	712952
8.	Burdwan	5015	618695
9.	Malda	2688	596162
	Total	**27917**	**3628417**

5

Impact of the Scheme

The Mid-day Meal Scheme not only promotes enrolment of the students but also develop habit among the children to go schools everyday where they get guarantee of food at least one time a day which is difficult for the parents to manage due to poverty and economic constraints. This scheme develops enthusiasm among the children and reduces burden of the parents who are unable to send children to schools and rather utilising them as mode of income. This scheme gives economic relief to the parents. This study finds that because of implementation of the scheme the enrolment in the sample schools have constantly improved and children inclined to perform good result. The drop-out rate has come down to great extent. The performance in terms of result, it is observed that most of the students have been promoted in higher class as policy formulated by the Government not to fail students which discontinue them from the elementary education. This uplifts interest among the children and by and large they developed healthy practices of discipline like maintain queue while collecting food, wash hands, plate, glass, intake food on one platform without bothering social issues.

The following tables show enrolments, drop-outs and results of the students; mandal (Andhra Pradesh), block (Tamil Nadu, Himachal Pradesh, Uttar Pradesh and West Bengal) and taluk-wise (Gujarat). This study covers 240 schools of which 60 schools (20 each from Tamil Nadu, Gujarat and Himachal Pradesh) and 180 schools (60 each from Andhra Pradesh, Uttar Pradesh and West Bengal) taken into the samples.

TAMIL NADU

Table 5.1: Enrolment, drop-out and result of the sample schools in block Uthirameruru, district Kanchipuram, Tamil Nadu

		Enrolment of the students			
Class	*2001-02*	*2002-03*	*2003-04*	*2004-05*	*2005-06*
I	352	329	237	239	256
II	366	324	376	282	239
III	381	414	306	273	293
IV	336	367	333	307	305
V	368	360	350	363	306
Total	**1803**	**1694**	**1602**	**1464**	**1399**
		Drop-out of the students			
Class	*2001-02*	*2002-03*	*2003-04*	*2004-05*	*2005-06*
I	—	—	—	—	—
II	—	—	—	—	—
III	—	—	—	—	—
IV	—	—	—	—	—
V	—	—	—	—	—
Total	**—**	**—**	**—**	**—**	**—**
		Result of the students			
Class	*2001-02*	*2002-03*	*2003-04*	*2004-05*	*2005-06*
I	299	303	277	235	250
II	314	297	313	276	243
III	349	314	290	301	287
IV	308	348	284	306	302
V	336	306	362	327	313
Total	**1606**	**1568**	**1526**	**1145**	**1395**

Note: (—) symbol shows no drop-out.

Table 5.2 : Enrolment, drop-out and result of the sample schools in block Thripurar, district Kanchipuram, Tamil Nadu

Enrolment of the students

Class	*2001-02*	*2002-03*	*2003-04*	*2004-05*	*2005-06*
I	387	353	263	259	315
II	311	343	319	313	280
III	378	460	349	325	304
IV	416	357	404	322	303
V	284	384	392	389	334
Total	**1836**	**1897**	**1727**	**1608**	**1536**

Drop-out of the students

Class	*2001-02*	*2002-03*	*2003-04*	*2004-05*	*2005-06*
I	—	—	—	20	—
II	—	—	—	—	01
III	—	—	—	—	—
IV	—	—	—	—	—
V	—	—	—	—	—
Total	**—**	**—**	**—**	**02**	**01**

Result of the students

Class	*2001-02*	*2002-03*	*2003-04*	*2004-05*	*2005-06*
I	385	353	263	257	315
II	311	343	319	313	279
III	378	460	349	325	304
IV	416	357	404	322	303
V	284	384	392	389	334
Total	**1774**	**1897**	**1727**	**1606**	**1535**

GUJARAT

Table 5.3: Enrolment, drop-out and result of the sample schools in taluk Himatnagar, district Himatnagar, Gujarat

Enrolment of the students					
Class	*2001-02*	*2002-03*	*2003-04*	*2004-05*	*2005-06*
I	443	440	423	400	458
II	454	468	416	427	377
III	422	450	428	413	417
IV	382	387	424	451	407
V	296	294	331	396	367
Total	**2047**	**2039**	**2072**	**2087**	**2026**
Drop-out of the students					
Class	*2001-02*	*2002-03*	*2003-04*	*2004-05*	*2005-06*
I	—	—	—	—	—
II	—	—	—	—	—
III	—	—	—	—	—
IV	—	—	—	—	—
V	—	—	—	—	—
Total	**—**	**—**	**—**	**—**	**—**
Result of the students					
Class	*2001-02*	*2002-03*	*2003-04*	*2004-05*	*2005-06*
I	401	392	395	257	404
II	289	423	392	396	341
III	385	404	447	397	371
IV	307	368	407	421	388
V	295	267	311	368	340
Total	**1650**	**1863**	**1952**	**1839**	**1844**

Table 5.4: Enrolment, drop-out and result of the sample schools in taluk Bhiloda, district Himatnagar, Gujarat

		Enrolment of the students			
Class	*2001-02*	*2002-03*	*2003-04*	*2004-05*	*2005-06*
I	227	284	267	261	263
II	263	237	264	230	246
III	285	244	229	266	214
IV	273	286	250	239	254
V	310	332	306	281	254
Total	**1358**	**1383**	**1316**	**1277**	**1231**
		Drop-out of the students			
Class	*2001-02*	*2002-03*	*2003-04*	*2004-05*	*2005-06*
I	—	—	—	—	—
II	—	—	—	—	—
III	—	—	—	—	—
IV	—	—	—	—	—
V	—	—	—	—	—
Total	**—**	**—**	**—**	**—**	**—**
		Result of the students			
Class	*2001-02*	*2002-03*	*2003-04*	*2004-05*	*2005-06*
I	228	259	222	218	227
II	227	206	237	196	206
III	257	273	204	222	205
IV	268	256	201	201	221
V	260	276	237	228	216
Total	**1240**	**1270**	**1101**	**1065**	**1075**

HIMACHAL PRADESH

Table 5.5: Enrolment, drop-out and result of the sample schools in block Gumarwin-I, district Bilaspur, Himachal Pradesh

Enrolment of the students					
Class	*2001-02*	*2002-03*	*2003-04*	*2004-05*	*2005-06*
I	198	175	141	157	122
II	158	171	170	140	150
III	188	163	163	176	137
IV	179	175	178	177	172
V	205	194	164	169	177
Total	**928**	**878**	**816**	**819**	**663**
Drop-out of the students					
Class	*2001-02*	*2002-03*	*2003-04*	*2004-05*	*2005-06*
I	—	—	—	—	—
II	—	—	—	—	—
III	—	—	—	—	—
IV	—	—	—	—	—
V	—	—	—	—	—
Total	**—**	**—**	**—**	**—**	**—**
Result of the students					
Class	*2001-02*	*2002-03*	*2003-04*	*2004-05*	*2005-06*
I	189	170	141	90	131
II	156	171	170	144	137
III	184	161	163	176	142
IV	174	175	164	173	171
V	203	181	168	161	176
Total	**906**	**858**	**806**	**744**	**756**

Table 5.6: Enrolment, drop-out and result of the sample schools in block Gumarwin-II, district Bilaspur, Himachal Pradesh

Enrolment of the students					
Class	*2001-02*	*2002-03*	*2003-04*	*2004-05*	*2005-06*
I	115	127	113	106	99
II	94	103	108	105	88
III	104	93	94	105	97
IV	116	113	95	102	102
V	130	117	105	88	92
Total	**559**	**553**	**515**	**506**	**475**
Drop-out of the students					
Class	*2001-02*	*2002-03*	*2003-04*	*2004-05*	*2005-06*
I	—	—	—	—	—
II	—	—	—	—	—
III	—	—	—	—	—
IV	—	—	—	—	—
V	—	—	—	—	—
Total	**—**	**—**	**—**	**—**	**—**
Result of the students					
Class	*2001-02*	*2002-03*	*2003-04*	*2004-05*	*2005-06*
I	105	111	109	99	94
II	84	97	91	105	84
III	98	95	88	99	84
IV	116	105	76	88	102
V	123	109	95	88	90
Total	**526**	**632**	**459**	**479**	**454**

ANDHRA PRADESH

Table 5.7: Enrolment, drop-out and result of the sample schools in mandal Valigonda, district Nalgonda, Andhra Pradesh

Enrolment of the students						
Class	*2001-02*	*2002-03*	*2003-04*	*2004-05*	*2005-06*	*2006-07*
I	521	448	407	359	355	338
II	507	438	427	314	299	316
III	514	547	471	392	323	324
IV	484	522	571	426	390	336
V	474	553	547	548	431	408
Total	**2500**	**2508**	**2423**	**2039**	**1798**	**1722**
Drop-out of the students						
Class	*2001-02*	*2002-03*	*2003-04*	*2004-05*	*2005-06*	*2006-07*
I	—	—	—	6	2	5
II	1	6	1	1	—	1
III	3	—	2	—	—	—
IV	2	—	2	2	—	—
V	2	—	—	—	—	—
Total	**8**	**6**	**5**	**9**	**2**	**6**
Result of the students						
Class	*2001-02*	*2002-03*	*2003-04*	*2004-05*	*2005-06*	*2006-07*
I	519	436	426	314	298	315
II	506	436	426	314	298	315
III	511	547	468	392	323	324
IV	482	522	570	427	388	335
V	473	553	547	548	430	407
Total	**2491**	**2494**	**2437**	**1995**	**1737**	**1696**

Table 5.8: Enrolment, drop-out and result of the sample schools in mandal Baptla, district Guntur, Andhra Pradesh

Enrolment of the students						
Class	*2001-02*	*2002-03*	*2003-04*	*2004-05*	*2005-06*	*2006-07*
I	462	449	431	362	444	494
II	485	512	421	447	402	410
III	469	463	468	419	481	425
IV	456	441	362	445	421	462
V	416	455	384	392	427	416
Total	**2288**	**2320**	**2066**	**2065**	**2175**	**2207**
Drop-out of the students						
Class	2001-02	2002-03	2003-04	2004-05	2005-06	2006-07
I	7	16	8	9	21	24
II	7	28	1	5	17	5
III	3	31	2	1	7	9
IV	2	32	5	5	10	21
V	1	41	3	3	3	5
Total	**20**	**148**	**19**	**23**	**58**	**64**
Result of the students						
Class	*2001-02*	*2002-03*	*2003-04*	*2004-05*	*2005-06*	*2006-07*
I	412	412	385	329	417	435
II	450	484	397	405	403	384
III	430	452	452	416	449	430
IV	443	421	353	439	407	455
V	413	447	376	386	424	409
Total	**2148**	**2216**	**1963**	**1975**	**2100**	**2113**

Table 5.9: Enrolment, drop-out and result of the sample schools in mandal Irla, district Rayalaseema, Andhra Pradesh

			Enrolment of the students			
Class	*2001-02*	*2002-03*	*2003-04*	*2004-05*	*2005-06*	*2006-07*
I	249	224	264	194	223	206
II	259	249	233	261	195	213
III	305	263	246	229	255	195
IV	302	280	261	243	223	246
V	281	286	285	260	241	223
Total	**1396**	**1302**	**1289**	**1187**	**1137**	**1083**
			Drop-out of the students			
Class	*2001-02*	*2002-03*	*2003-04*	*2004-05*	*2005-06*	*2006-07*
I	1	1	—	1	2	—
II	—	1	—	3	1	1
III	—	—	1	1	—	—
IV	1	6	—	—	—	—
V	1	1	—	—	—	—
Total	**3**	**9**	**1**	**5**	**3**	**1**
			Result of the students			
Class	*2001-02*	*2002-03*	*2003-04*	*2004-05*	*2005-06*	*2006-07*
I	249	221	262	194	221	207
II	260	248	234	258	195	212
III	305	263	246	229	254	195
IV	304	274	261	243	223	246
V	281	285	285	260	241	223
Total	**1399**	**1291**	**1288**	**1184**	**1134**	**1083**

UTTAR PRADESH

Table 5.10: Enrolment, drop-out and result of the sample schools in block Behjan, district Lakhimpur Kheri, Uttar Pradesh

Enrolment of the students						
Class	*2001-02*	*2002-03*	*2003-04*	*2004-05*	*2005-06*	*2006-07*
I	646	813	909	1015	857	962
II	855	719	853	960	1003	927
III	849	739	739	911	1008	1005
IV	678	672	710	646	853	942
V	616	561	633	598	604	771
Total	**3644**	**3504**	**3844**	**4130**	**4325**	**4607**
Drop-out of the students						
Class	*2001-02*	*2002-03*	*2003-04*	*2004-05*	*2005-06*	*2006-07*
I	38	37	55	50	30	40
II	81	47	39	17	32	31
III	62	27	66	39	22	41
IV	51	52	40	28	27	36
V	51	37	27	9	40	29
Total	**283**	**200**	**227**	**143**	**151**	**177**
Result of the students						
Class	*2001-02*	*2002-03*	*2003-04*	*2004-05*	*2005-06*	*2006-07*
I	590	735	837	956	813	888
II	749	647	807	931	976	869
III	754	666	674	851	933	924
IV	634	600	666	597	796	877
V	566	534	607	582	547	732
Total	**3293**	**3182**	**3591**	**3917**	**4065**	**4290**

Table 5.11: Enrolment, drop-out and result of the sample schools in block Soran, district Allahabad, Uttar Pradesh

			Enrolment of the students			
Class	*2001-02*	*2002-03*	*2003-04*	*2004-05*	*2005-06*	*2006-07*
I	1095	1484	1462	1166	990	1241
II	861	1191	1308	1303	1000	927
III	741	853	1094	1296	1072	905
IV	511	730	883	994	1031	912
V	650	491	653	718	870	879
Total	**3858**	**4749**	**5400**	**5477**	**4963**	**4864**
			Drop-out of the students			
Class	*2001-02*	*2002-03*	*2003-04*	*2004-05*	*2005-06*	*2006-07*
I	22	25	57	124	35	126
II	27	129	55	147	85	73
III	14	47	36	110	110	76
IV	11	50	78	125	58	87
V	22	22	53	55	103	142
Total	**96**	**273**	**279**	**561**	**391**	**504**
			Result of the students			
Class	*2001-02*	*2002-03*	*2003-04*	*2004-05*	*2005-06*	*2006-07*
I	1126	1388	1343	1035	965	1045
II	895	1097	1258	1092	933	814
III	751	865	1097	1152	1095	798
IV	495	701	834	940	994	854
V	628	482	606	651	771	726
Total	**3895**	**4533**	**5138**	**4870**	**4758**	**4237**

Note: In Allahabad district 3 Primary Schools (namely: Bhadri, Dadupur and Bhavapur) out of a sample of 20 schools, had not furnished data on above.

Table 5.12: Enrolment, drop-out and result of the sample schools in block Chirala, district Jhansi, Uttar Pradesh

Enrolment of the students						
Class	*2001-02*	*2002-03*	*2003-04*	*2004-05*	*2005-06*	*2006-07*
I	571	547	520	418	504	577
II	513	554	575	530	447	514
III	424	515	554	566	528	455
IV	427	406	489	547	547	477
V	357	406	396	480	520	515
Total	**2292**	**2428**	**2534**	**2541**	**2546**	**2538**
Drop-out of the students						
Class	*2001-02*	*2002-03*	*2003-04*	*2004-05*	*2005-06*	*2006-07*
I	14	1	—	—	3	—
II	1	19	—	—	1	26
III	1	1	21	—	4	7
IV	3	1	10	21	27	1
V	—	2	2	1	21	7
Total	**19**	**24**	**33**	**22**	**56**	**41**
Result of the students						
Class	*2001-02*	*2002-03*	*2003-04*	*2004-05*	*2005-06*	*2006-07*
I	532	552	555	419	471	574
II	521	519	564	573	453	473
III	419	510	520	547	563	472
IV	381	392	495	510	535	504
V	364	371	382	451	486	506
Total	**2217**	**2344**	**2516**	**2500**	**2508**	**2529**

WEST BENGAL

Table 5.13: Enrolment, drop-out and result of the sample schools in block Barrackpur-II, district North 24 Parganas, West Bengal

Enrolment of the students						
Class	*2001-02*	*2002-03*	*2003-04*	*2004-05*	*2005-06*	*2006-07*
I	561	971	956	1014	971	980
II	484	935	889	842	921	865
III	488	911	918	884	799	1000
IV	431	774	751	750	824	693
V	53	27	103	145	145	192
Total	**2017**	**3618**	**3617**	**3635**	**3660**	**3730**
Drop-out of the students						
Class	*2001-02*	*2002-03*	*2003-04*	*2004-05*	*2005-06*	*2006-07*
I	—	36	25	17	13	9
II	—	9	6	—	3	3
III	—	12	3	6	3	12
IV	—	9	3	6	9	6
V	—	—	16	6	7	8
Total	**—**	**66**	**53**	**35**	**35**	**38**
Result of the students						
Class	*2001-02*	*2002-03*	*2003-04*	*2004-05*	*2005-06*	*2006-07*
I	553	926	903	989	947	959
II	477	919	893	833	907	857
III	483	892	911	872	790	977
IV	430	763	748	742	815	684
V	—	—	80	103	143	243
Total	**1943**	**3500**	**3535**	**3539**	**3602**	**3720**

Table 5.14: Enrolment, drop-out and result of the sample schools in block Kanksa, district Burdwan, West Bengal

Enrolment of the students						
Class	*2001-02*	*2002-03*	*2003-04*	*2004-05*	*2005-06*	*2006-07*
I	1039	866	1015	880	838	875
II	773	868	723	862	699	743
III	975	700	787	668	812	689
IV	753	826	708	815	629	782
V	368	344	392	354	393	323
Total	**3908**	**3604**	**3625**	**3579**	**3371**	**3412**
Drop-out of the students						
Class	*2001-02*	*2002-03*	*2003-04*	*2004-05*	*2005-06*	*2006-07*
I	25	38	33	38	29	16
II	6	15	24	31	35	24
III	37	11	38	9	19	18
IV	4	52	33	4	25	19
V	—	—	—	—	—	—
Total	**72**	**116**	**128**	**82**	**108**	**77**
Result of the students						
Class	*2001-02*	*2002-03*	*2003-04*	*2004-05*	*2005-06*	*2006-07*
I	899	740	899	768	755	787
II	721	845	708	847	694	727
III	845	682	786	657	797	683
IV	699	816	696	808	622	770
V	368	344	392	354	393	323
Total	**3532**	**3427**	**3481**	**3434**	**3261**	**3290**

Table 5.15: Enrolment, drop-out and result of the sample schools in block Ratua, district Malda, West Bengal

Enrolment of the students						
Class	*2001-02*	*2002-03*	*2003-04*	*2004-05*	*2005-06*	*2006-07*
I	2289	2551	3248	2700	2439	2319
II	1350	1496	1567	1639	1743	1779
III	1040	1241	1359	1434	1454	1432
IV	1022	1070	1182	1197	1404	1443
V	—	—	—	—	—	—
Total	**5701**	**6358**	**7356**	**6970**	**7040**	**6973**
Drop-out of the students						
Class	*2001-02*	*2002-03*	*2003-04*	*2004-05*	*2005-06*	*2006-07*
I	140	149	137	144	158	159
II	50	57	75	55	78	122
III	60	46	35	68	66	76
IV	62	54	40	86	71	106
V	—	—	—	—	—	—
Total	**312**	**306**	**287**	**353**	**373**	**463**
Result of the students						
Class	*2001-02*	*2002-03*	*2003-04*	*2004-05*	*2005-06*	*2006-07*
I	1628	1925	2202	2006	1734	1600
II	1163	1241	1346	1355	1391	1194
III	933	1125	1197	1238	1347	1050
IV	830	989	1115	990	1259	1063
V	—	—	—	—	—	—
Total	**4554**	**5280**	**5860**	**5589**	**5731**	**4907**

Note: In the school 5th class was existed when this study was carried out.

The above tables show enrolment, drop-out and result of the student class-wise in sample schools of all the six States from last five years from the year of conducting study. In case of Tamil Nadu, Gujarat and Himachal Pradesh where this study was conducted in 2006 where the data of enrolment, drop-out and result has been gathered from 2001-02 to 2005-06 whereas in Andhra Pradesh, Uttar Pradesh and West Bengal this study was conducted in 2007, therefore, the data of enrolment, drop-out and result has been collected from 2002-03 to 2006-07. The above tables show that in sample schools Uthirameruru block the drop-out has not been recorded whereas in sample schools of Thripurar block the drop-out has been found nominal in 2004-05 and 2005-06. In sample schools of Gujarat and Himachal Pradesh the drop-out has not been found. In Andhra Pradesh the drop-out found higher in sample schools of Guntur district (coastal Andhra) compared to other two reasons. In Uttar Pradesh, drop-out ratio is higher in Lakhimpur Kehri and Allahabad than Jhansi district.

Similarly, in West Bengal the drop-out found higher in Malwa district compared to Burdwan and North 24 Parganas districts. This study finds that the drop-out rate is higher where the agriculture is predominant. Guntur in Andhra Pradesh, Lakhimpur Kehri and Allahabad districts in Uttar Pradesh and Malda in West Bengal are ahead in agriculture where drop-out found higher compared to other districts of the same State. The parents give priority on agriculture wage rather than realize importance of the education. In addition to this, migration of the parents which is higher in Bundelkhand and Telengana regions affect education of the children. Allahabad which is a centre of academic institutions could not control the drop-out rate. It is brought to the notice that now most of the parents who are keen for the education of their children send their children to the private schools. In case of rural areas this factor has become popular among the conscious parents. The teachers who posted in the Government schools even had not put their children in the Government schools due to lack of proper infrastructure, lack of dedicated teaching staff, influence of English, etc. A small section of the parents, students and teachers however informed that due to indiscipline in functioning of the scheme and workload on teachers, they are not able to complete syllabus in time. Students could not concentrate on education rather than keep eyes on kitchen to get food. Few parents however, revealed that their children lose interest in education due to unscheduled supply of food in the schools. Therefore, they prefer those schools where teacher justified their role.

The guidelines of the scheme indicates that teacher should pay attention on education whereas scheme's work should be handed over to the staff such as organizer, cook, helper who are responsible for the function of the scheme but it is noticed that without involvement of the teacher from one to other angle this scheme could not run smoothly until and unless Tamil Nadu model could not be established. Gujarat has followed the same model but other States are still lagging behind to hand over complete task to the employee work under the scheme. In Tamil Nadu this scheme has been influenced by the political parties and whoever comes in the power supplement additional nutrition in form of eggs which is sometimes difficult to get in market due to high demand. Supplies of the eggs twice to thrice a week attract students to come over school regularly.

The Village Education Committees which formed under the provision of Sarva Shiksha Abhiyan (SSA) play active role to promote enrolment of the students. Committee members discuss this issue in its meeting.

6

Findings and Recommendations

Education is root of modernization and human development. Education cuts across three dimensions such as economic, cultural and political, which are considered the measuring roots of development process. Education is a learning process and which continues throughout the life. Education is helpful to lift people above the crude human life and create modern thought. Education promotes mobilization and encourages people to participate in development activities. Education makes people skilled towards jobs and creates atmosphere for better productivity.

To promote education, Government of India grants financial assistance and loan to the States and Union Territories on different aspects such as opening and maintenance of ashram schools, arrange hostel facilities, organizing and developing teaching materials, awarding stipends, provide reading and writing materials, provide uniforms and dress to the students, exempting Scheduled Caste and Scheduled Tribe candidates from tuition fee, providing mid-day meals, sanction scholarship both pre- and post-matric to the students whose parents are unable to meet the expenditure of education.

The National Programme of Nutritional support to Primary Education popularly known as Mid-Day Meal Scheme has been launched on 15th August, 1995 at national level. This programme intended to give a boost to universalization of primary education by increasing enrolment, retention and attendance, and simultaneously impacting upon nutritional status to the students in primary classes. This scheme involved provision of lunch free of cost to school children in all the working days. This scheme gives great relief to the parents who are economically not sound and who promote children for labour to meet necessity of the family.

Prior to implementation at national level, this scheme was running in tribal areas of Madhya Pradesh and Orissa, to promote education among the tribal children. By 1990-91, this scheme has been implemented by many of the states such as Madhya Pradesh, Kerala, Maharashtra, Meghalaya, Mizoram, Nagaland, Goa, Sikkim, etc. This scheme has been functioning in Tamil Nadu, Gujarat, Kerala and Union Territory of Pondichery even prior to 1995 when the Government of India announces at national level. Of course, the history of Mid-Day Meals in Tamil Nadu is very old and it was started in 1923 for disadvantaged children in Madras Municipal Corporation, later on this scheme was stopped. But again this scheme was reintroduced on July 1, 1982 by M.G. Ramchandran then the Chief Minister of State.

This programme was initially implemented in child welfare centres in rural areas for the pre-school children in the age group of 2-5 years, and for primary school children in the age group of 8-9 years. The benefit of the scheme has now been expanded up to the middle class students. Till December 2006, this scheme was running in 41344 centres covering 58.75 lakh students from Class I to Class VIII. Class I to V expenditure borne by Government of India, whereas VI to VIII expenditure borne by the State Government. This scheme runs by the Social Welfare Department when and then Dravidum Mungdam Kangdam (DMK) rule in the State whereas All India Adi Dravidum Mungdam Kangdam (AIADMK) run this scheme through the Rural Development Department.

In Gujarat, this scheme came into existent from middle of 1980s. Till December 2006, this scheme has been implemented in 29990 centres covering 46.78 lakh students from class I to VII, the expenditure of upto class V is borne by Government of India whereas for the students of VI to VII classes, expenditure borne by the State Government. The provision of supply cooked food in Gujarat began since November 17, 1984. Prior to this, students were getting foodgrains of 3 kg per month per head.

In Himachal Pradesh, this scheme implemented since August 15, 1995. In initial state, this scheme was launched in 18 community development blocks then it has been extended in 32 community development blocks but now this scheme has been functioning in all the 72 community development blocks of the state. Prior to May 21, 2003, students used to get 3 kg of rice per head per month. In December 2006, this scheme was running in 10610 centres with the coverage of 24.77 lakhs students. In Himachal Pradesh, this scheme was implemented for the primary school children. This scheme also covers students of Government schools, Government aided primary schools, and schools which run by the local bodies.

For monitoring the scheme, committees are constituted at various levels such as Centre, State, District, Taluk or Block and Gram Panchayat level. All these committees organize meetings and review progress of the scheme in time, and simultaneously make suitable suggestions for better implementation of the scheme. Members of all committees monitor the functions of the scheme.

The Gram Panchayat Level Committee consists of President (GP), Head of the school (Head Master or Head Mistress), Village Administrative Officer, Organizer, representative of Parent Teacher Association (PTA), representative of Mother Teacher Association (MTA), representative of Self-Help Group, prestigious persons of village, etc. The structure of Gram Panchayat Level Committee differs from one to other area studied. This committee works under the Chairmanship of President, Gram Panchayat. This committee being close to grassroots monitoring functions of the scheme closely. The members of this committee spread message of the education and propagate provision of the scheme among the parents, and simultaneously encourage parents, so parents send their children to school. The members of this committee sort out problems locally and create atmosphere for clean and hygienic environment in and around the schools.

In Tamil Nadu, this scheme is run by Social Welfare Department whereas in Gujarat this scheme is run by Commissioner Mid-Day Meals and Schools. In Himachal

Pradesh, Director Elementary Education is the nodal agency at state level. At grassroots level, this scheme implemented by the organizers, cook and helpers. All these employees get remuneration on consolidated basis by the above departments. The Government of Tamil Nadu pay scale as well as consolidated salary to the organizers, whereas Government of Gujarat pay consolidated remuneration to all who involved in different forms like organizers and helpers. In Andhra Pradesh, Uttar Pradesh and West Bengal this scheme has been launched since August 15, 1995. In Andhra Pradesh, Uttar Pradesh and West Bengal this scheme is run by the education department. In Andhra Pradesh and West Bengal members of self-help groups take care for preparing and supplying of food to the students whereas in Uttar Pradesh, Pradhan of Gram Panchayat runs scheme through the help of cook for which Pradhan pays consolidated remuneration of Rs. 500 per month.

Objectives of the Study

- To understand the variance of administrative structure for implementation of the scheme in different states and a comparative effectiveness of the structure,
- To examine the extent of involvement and contributions of various local institutions in implementation of the scheme,
- To examine the problem in proper implementation of the scheme, and
- To make suitable suggestions for further improvement in functioning of the scheme.

Methodology

This study has been carried out in two consecutive years, i.e. 2006-07 and 2007-08. In 2006-07, Tamil Nadu, Gujarat and Himachal Pradesh were selected whereas in 2007-08, Andhra Pradesh, Uttar Pradesh and West Bengal were chosen. In Tamil Nadu, Uthirameruru and Thirupurar blocks of Kanchipuram district were selected whereas in Gujarat, Himatnagar and

Bhiloda of Sabarkanta district were chosen. In Himachal Pradesh, Gumarwin I and Gumarwin II of Bilaspur district were selected. In each district two blocks (in case of Gujarat—taluk) were chosen. Further, from each district, 20 schools were chosen which means total 60 schools were chosen from three States—Tamil Nadu, Gujarat and Himachal Pradesh.

In 2007-08, the sample size has been increased from 20 to 60 with consistence of 20 schools reason-wise. The logic behind this was to understand function of the scheme region-wise because each State has its geographical and cultural variation. Keeping in view, the samples have been drawn region-wise in Andhra Pradesh, Uttar Pradesh and West Bengal.

In Andhra Pradesh, Valigonda mandal of Nalgonda district (Telengana region), Baptla mandal of Guntur district (Coastal region) and Irla mandal of Chittoor district (Rayalaseema) were chosen. Similarly, in Uttar Pradesh, Behjan block of Lakhimpur Kheri district, Soran block of Allahabad district and Chirgaon block of Jhansi district were chosen. In West Bengal, Barrackpur II, Kanksa and Ratua blocks were chosen simultaneously from North 24 Parganas, Burdwan and Malda districts. The selection of schools, blocks and districts were made based on performance of the scheme and impact of the scheme region-wise. Total 180 schools were chosen from all the three States—Andhra Pradesh, Uttar Pradesh and West Bengal. This study covers all together 240 schools from all the six States.

This study covers different aspects like functions of the committees which constituted at state, district, block and gram panchayat level. On the other side, this study concentrates on role and functions of nodal department especially at grassroots level where this scheme has been implementing. This study focuses on monitoring mechanism of the scheme along with other relevant issues like availability of infrastructural facilities to the school premises, coverage of enrolment, retention, drop-out and results of the students from last five years to understand the function and impact of the scheme. In Andhra Pradesh mandals have been created after bifurcation of the blocks which makes Government machineries accessible to the people.

Findings

Mid-Day Meals Scheme is one of the ambitious schemes, which promotes enthusiasm for educational development among the children especially whose parents are economically poor and socially disadvantaged. This scheme promotes enrolment of the students, retains them in schools and reduce drop-out of those children whose parents have got poor socio-economic background. This scheme helps to eliminate child labour system and stop migration of children along with the parents.

Enrolment and Performance

This study finds that this scheme helps to improve enrolment of the students constantly and reduced drop-out rate among the students. Similarly, results of the students have improved in sample schools of all the six states. This scheme spreads the message of education development. This scheme has become popular among the children and the parents who are unable to meet costs of the education, and who take children with them to urban or semi-urban areas for employment opportunities. This scheme reduces migration of the children along with the parents which make them to work on places like hotels, restaurants, garages, manufacturing units of crackers, bar, brick kiln, etc. on low wages. Due to implementation of this scheme enrolment of the students and performance in the forms of result both have constantly increased but due to control over birth rate (which is negligible) especially among the middle and upper middle class families in rural area, and accessibility of schools, the enrolment is constant in many of the sample schools and the same continue next year in higher class (until and unless child would not drop the school due to one or other reason).

It is noticed especially in higher class, when student leave the school, the strength of the students for the next year would slightly move up and down otherwise in general, no much flexibility has been recorded in enrolment. The benefit of the scheme initiate from the day when one student attends the school and continue till the schooling. The flow of enrolment could be seen only in the beginning and which continue with little up and down. In many sample schools, the result has been found cent-per-cent which was maintained as the Government instructions that child could not discontinue school due to poor performance in examinations. The motto of Government is to promote education up to the age of 14 years, which is otherwise declared as the Right of Child as per the instructions given by the Hon'ble Supreme Court.

The drop-out, in general found very low in many sample schools except sample schools of Uttar Pradesh and West Bengal. The drop-out vary from region to region. The drop-out was active in sample schools of Coastal belt of Andhra Pradesh (Guntur district), North and South-Eastern belt (Lakhimpur Kheri and Allahabad districts), and Central and middle belt (Burdwan and Malda districts) which got fertile land and due to that parents and children both get employment in agriculture and its allied activities whereas drop-out rate was low in the rest of study areas.

Desperate Attitude

One observation has been made that now many of the parents even in rural areas too realized importance of the education and would like to send their children in better schools preferably with English medium. Even some of the teachers who work in the sample schools had put their children in other schools where education is better though they belong to the same locality. On other side, a small group of the teachers who engaged in dealing of the scheme, however, brought to notice that due to implementation of the scheme they are unable to complete syllabus in time, and according to them enrolment has not increased because of the scheme but now most of the parents realize importance of education, therefore, they send their children to the schools.

It is brought to the notice that students belonging to well families, who happen to take lunch at home, however, informed that they are bound to wait for the next session till the lunch is not completed by the beneficiaries of the scheme. The parents of such students have also developed the same notion. These thoughts emerged among those students and parents who are keen on education. Inconsistency of lunch hours affects schedule of the academic session. In Uttar Pradesh, Chapattis serves twice in a week, which needs more time for its preparation especially where students enrolment is higher. In most of the schools, where numerical strength of the students is high, they take food in the class rooms itself which required additional time to clean floor.

Supply of Foodgrains and Financial Assistance

The Government of India supplies foodgrains through various channels from State Food Corporation Department to fair price shop of Gram Panchayat. There is a provision to store foodgrains at district/taluk/block level godown. In Tamil Nadu, the foodgrains are supplied at schools whereas in Gujarat and Himachal Pradesh, the foodgrains are collected by the engaged staff from fair price shops. In Gujarat, this responsibility has been given to the organizer who is employee of the scheme on part-time basis whereas in Himachal Pradesh (due to non-existing of organizer post) concerned teacher is bound to lift foodgrains from the fair price shops. In this process, teacher has to pay high transportation cost. The transportation cost for carrying foodgrains to the school vary from one to other place and which change timely when the prices of diesel or petrol fluctuate. This creates difficulty for the teachers.

Besides, foodgrains, Government of India furnishes financial assistance in form of convergence cost at the rate of one rupee and fifty paisa per child per school day. This expenditure fulfils the cost of vegetables, contingents, fuel, edible oil, salt, transportation (from fair price shop to school), stationery, etc. The Government of Tamil Nadu contributes 0.35 paisa per student per school day. The reason behind such low assistance is that, the Government of Tamil Nadu supplies oil, salt, contingents, etc. at the door of school along with the foodgrains. The Government of Tamil Nadu merges Central funds into the state and reallocates funds at the rate of 0.35 paisa per student per school day. The Government of Gujarat contributes 70 paisa in case of per student per school day whereas Government of Himachal Pradesh pays 1.00 rupee per student per school day for making scheme healthy.

The Government of Himachal Pradesh provides Mid-Day Meals up to primary level students as per the norms of Government of India whereas Government of Tamil Nadu and Government of Gujarat cover students simultaneously up to middle and upper primary levels. The additional cost for running the scheme is borne by concerned State Government both in terms of cost of foodgrains and disbursement of financial cost. In Himachal Pradesh, foodgrains supply based on availability of the stock with the fair price shop. This leads problem for the implementing agency to supply food to the student according to prescribed guidelines. As per the guidelines, the Government of India supplies foodgrains for 200 days to each State whereas beyond 200 days, the concerned State Government has to arrange with their own allocation. In Tamil Nadu and Gujarat, most of the sample schools use firewood for cooking whereas in Himachal Pradesh almost all the schools have got gas connection accept one. The gas connection has been made by Sarva Siksha Abhiyan (SSA).

The Government of West Bengal also covers primary schools like Government of Himachal Pradesh with the contribution of Government of India whereas Government of Uttar Pradesh and Government of Andhra Pradesh cover students up to upper primary and beyond primary for which the cost is borne by State Governments. In all the six States, foodgrains supply well in advance. Almost all the sample schools use firewood for cooking the food. In Andhra Pradesh, the foodgrains supplied by the Government of India at the nearest godowns and from the godowns the foodgrains is lifted by the local distributors who make arrangement of supplying foodgrains to the schools. In Uttar Pradesh, foodgrains keep in the house of Pradhan (President of Gram Panchayat) whereas in West Bengal, foodgrains is routed through various channels from district to Gram Panchayat. Besides, foodgrains,

Government of India contributes financial assistance in form of convergence cost at the rate of one rupee fifty paisa per child per school day. This expenditure fulfils the cost of vegetables, contingents, fuel, edible oil, salt, stationery, etc. The State Governments also make financial contribution for making scheme healthy. The Andhra Pradesh Government contributes 1.00 rupee, 75 paisa and 50 paisa according to strength of the students' school-wise. This range has divided into three categories; first range consist students up to 50 whereas second range covers strength of students between 50 and 100, and third one covers more than 100 students means wherever the strength of students is higher than 100 then State Government contributes at the rate of 0.50 paisa per student per day. The Government of Uttar Pradesh also contributes 0.50 paisa for each student each school day whereas Government of West Bengal pays Re. 1.00 per student per school day.

It is noticed that financial assistance is not reaching in time due to late submission of utilization by the schools as well flow of funds from to other channels. It is brought to notice that remuneration of engaged staff and amount of ingredients which is bought on credit get delays for three-four months. The engaged staff loose interest to run the scheme because of such problem. This problem is well aware about the members of other self-help groups and therefore, they would not like to run the scheme on rotation basis. In case of Andhra Pradesh, most of the young women belonging to different self-help groups prefer to work in agriculture fields due to high remuneration. It is brought to notice that potential age group get wages between Rs. 60 and 70 per day which is much higher than remuneration supposed to get from the scheme. As a result two or three old women get themselves involved with the scheme. The same scenario exists in Uttar Pradesh. In West Bengal, transfer of one to other group found active in case of running the scheme even though remuneration is low. As stated earlier that the Government of West Bengal, pays Rs. 600 remuneration which share by the women. The healthy participation by the members of self-help groups is not really boost the scheme but poverty and unemployment both equally responsible to motivate members to participate in the scheme. On the other side, caste factor demotivates women especially those who are belonging to socially deprived sections to participate in the scheme as the feudal aristocrats oppose involvement of those women in the cooking process. This system noticed in Andhra Pradesh, Tamil Nadu, Uttar Pradesh and even in Gujarat which is ahead in the process of industrialization.

Menu

The different types of food no doubt attract students. Before formulation of menu students were getting *khichadi* regularly which was demotivating students to attend school regular. Menu promotes attendance and attracts students to large extent. Menu differs from State to State which is decided by State Level Steering-*cum*-Monitoring Committee but simultaneously flexibility has also been given to District and Block Level Steering-*cum*-Monitoring Committees to promote menu according to local requirement or local dietary habit.

In Tamil Nadu, students get different types of food everyday such as on Monday students get rice, dal, one egg per head, Tuesday—rice and dal, Wednesday—rice, dal and one egg per head, Thursday—rice, dal and 20 grams Green gram or Bengali grams, Friday—rice, dal and 20 grams boiled potato to each student. In Tamil Nadu, few schools (centres) run on Saturday to promote continuity of the children.

In Gujarat, menu covers: Monday—Pulao (vegetable, rice), Tuesday—Muthiya (local diet), Wednesday—rice, dal/dhokri (local diet), Thursday—sukdi (local diet), Friday—Pulao.

In Himachal Pradesh, weekly menu covers: Monday—rice and dal, Tuesday—Mitha Bhat (sweet rice), Wednesday—Pulao (mixture of rice and vegetables), Thursday—rice and dal, Friday—pulao, and on Saturday—rice and dal.

In Andhra Pradesh, students get rice and sambhar (mixed vegetables in dal) everyday along with the eggs on Monday and Wednesday. In the place of eggs, there is a provision of supplying banana or sweet in such schools which covered by International Society for Krishna Consciousness (ISKCON) and Kalahasti Temple Trust. Naandi Foundation, ISCON and Kalahasti Temple Trust covered a large number of schools in Andhra Pradesh. Naandi Foundation concentrates in twin city of Hyderabad and Secundrabad whereas ISKCON and Kalahasti Temple work in the rural areas.

In Uttar Pradesh, the menu covers: Monday—roti/puri with dal or vegetables (with Soyabean). Tuesday—rice and vegetables mixed dal, Wednesday—rice, kadi or mitha rice (sweet rice/kheer), Thursday—roti with vegetables mixed dal or puri along with vegetables and soyabean, Friday—Tahri, mitha rice or rice vegetables with soyabean.

In West Bengal, weekly menu covers: rice and dal (with mixed vegetables or soyabean) along with eggs on Monday and Friday. The above menu covers 100 grams rice, 15 grams dal, 50 grams vegetables, 5 grams oil, condiments, salt, etc. for per student per school day.

Health of the Students

This study finds that because of the implementation of the scheme the health condition of the children has improved to great extent. Children now do not get sick frequently and moreover, they get healthy and nutritious food at school which is hardly available at home especially students whose parents are facing poverty and migrate to urban and semi-urban areas for employment. This scheme promotes benefit for the children as well as reduces burden of the parents at least one time of a day. Children developed habit of washing hands and plates before and after the lunch which has reduced possibilities of falling them sick.

Discipline and Brotherhood Atmosphere

This scheme promotes discipline among the children. For collecting of food, and washing plates and glasses both before and after food they maintain queue and wait for their chance patiently. This study finds that this scheme develops brotherhood atmosphere among the children who sit below one roof and have lunch together without bothering caste and class prejudice. They pray commonly before taking food. But parents especially those who have developed feudal mind set oppose cook and helpers who belong to lower caste. This mind set has been noticed in few places in all the areas studied expect West Bengal.

Remuneration of Engaged Persons

In Uttar Pradesh, cooks get remuneration in form of consolidate salary of Rs. 500 per month. The cook is chosen by Pradhan (President of the Gram Panchayat). In all the States except Tamil Nadu, the organizers, cooks and helpers work on consolidated remuneration between Rs. 300 and Rs. 500. In Tamil Nadu and Gujarat, similar nature of mechanism has been adopted to run the scheme. In Tamil Nadu Organizers, Cooks and Helpers covered under the State pay scale whereas in Gujarat they get consolidated remuneration monthly. The remuneration in all the States depend on flow of fund except in Tamil Nadu where the remuneration is paid monthly in the form of salary. The State Government also pays remuneration from their own Budget to avoid delay as this scheme has become regular feature. In Andhra Pradesh, women share benefit out of convergence cost whereas in West Bengal, remuneration shares by the women out of Rs. 600 which they get from the State Government. In Andhra Pradesh, two or maximum three aged women involved in the scheme whereas young women would like to work in agriculture field as they get good remuneration. In West Bengal, groups are actively involved in running of the scheme and the rotation being made in time even within group or from one to other group. The remunerations of cooks and helpers is lower in Himachal Pradesh, Andhra Pradesh and Uttar Pradesh compared to Tamil Nadu, Gujarat and West Bengal. The remuneration is also not payed in time. In Andhra Pradesh engaged women make arrangement of remuneration from the convergence cost which is paid by the department.

Steering and Monitoring Committees

For better implementation of the scheme, a set of committees have been formed in all the six States. At State level, under the Chairmanship of Chief Secretary, a committee has been constituted, which consists different types of expertise. This committee schedules to organize its meeting once in six months but members of the committee in general do not assemble according to schedule until and unless major issue(s) do not emerge. But otherwise matter of the scheme discussed regularly every month under State level review committee, which attained by the representatives of different departments. State Level Steering-*cum*-Monitoring Committee organizes its meeting when need realize for specific reason like changing of menu, enhancement of price student-wise, coverage of more schools, enhance the remuneration of the organizers, cooks and helper. In such situation, members of the committee assemble under the Chairmanship of Chief Secretary. Similarly, at district, taluk/block levels similar types of committees have also been constituted to monitor function of the scheme timely. In Andhra Pradesh, Mandal Level Steering-*cum*-Monitoring Committee has been constituted at Mandal level which covers small areas then block. Roughly 3 or 4 mandals cover the area of one block. All above committees headed by different officers. At district level this committee is headed by the District Collector, at taluk level this committee is headed by the Taluk Development Officer (TDO), at block level this committee is headed by the Block Development Officer (BDO) whereas mandal level this committee is headed by the Mandal Development Officer (MDO).

The structure of Gram Panchayat Steering-*cum*-Monitoring Committee is differing from State to State. In Tamil Nadu, this committee functions under the Chairmanship of President (Gram Panchayats) with School Head Master (Member-Secretary), Village Administrative Officer, one representative of Self-Help Group, each one representative of Parent-Teacher Association, and Mother Teacher Association. In Gujarat, Gram Panchayat Steering-*cum*-Monitoring Committee consists of seven members in its body such as

President (Sarpanch) of the Gram Panchayat, Head Master (Member-Secretary), organizer (Mid-day Meal Scheme) and four prestigious persons of the village (which includes two women).

In Gumarwin-I and Gumarwin-II blocks of Bilaspur district in Himachal Pradesh, the Steering-*cum*-Monitoring Committee of Gram Panchayat comprises three to four members. In sample schools of Gumarwin-I block, the committee constituted with Pradhan (Sarpanch) of the Gram Panchayat, Head Master (Member-Secretary), one member of Mother-Teacher Association (MTA), and one member of Self-Help Groups. In sample schools of Gumarwin-II block, this committee comprises with Pradhan (Gram Panchayat), Head Master and representative of Mother-Teacher Association (MTA).

This study finds that in Tamil Nadu, Gram Panchayat Level Steering-*cum*-Monitoring Committee has been formed only in 3 schools out of 20 schools. In Gujarat, most of the schools have got this committee except two. In Himachal Pradesh, almost all sample schools have formed this committee but numerical strength of committee is not similar from one to other block and moreover, strength of the members is lower than Tamil Nadu and Gujarat. Of course, in Tamil Nadu, a large number of schools have not constituted this committee as per the guidelines of Government of India. In Gujarat and Himachal Pradesh, members of committees meet once in a month whereas in case of Tamil Nadu, question of holding meeting does not arise due to non-existent of the committee. But the President of Gram Panchayat visits centre on Independence and Republic Day and discuss various issues of village development which include school related matters.

Similarly, in Andhra Pradesh, Uttar Pradesh and West Bengal, the Gram Panchayat Level Steering-*cum*-Monitoring Committee was not formed but issues related of the scheme were discussed in the Village Education Committee (VEC) which formed by the Sarve Shiksha Abhiyan (SSA). The members of the Sarve Shiksha Abhiyan hold meeting regularly. The members of the SSA Committee in general, discuss issues of improving quality of food, ensure quantity of food with persuasion of guidelines, maintaining of clean and healthy environment in the school premises, supply of foodgrains, and ensure availability of safe drinking water, pursue that dogs should be kept away from the school boundary, construction of kitchen shed, promote enrolment especially girls, construction of rooms and boundary walls, recruit part-time teachers/Vidhya Volunteers, etc. including educational development of the village, promotes infrastructural facilities in the schools and promotes health of the students. The Village Education Committees function smoothly in all the six States. The members of the committees organize meetings regularly at least once in a month. The Village President holds position of Chairman of the Committee whereas School Head Master holds status of Member-Secretary. Apart from these, parents of students (both mother and father in equal number) become members the committee along with four prestigious persons of the village. The majority of the members in both of the committees, i.e. Village Education Committee and Mid-Day Meal Committee are moreover same hence; they give priority to the meeting of Sarve Shiksha Abhiyan (SSA) which is regular in nature. It is brought to the notice that more meeting affects livelihood pattern of the family as most of them depend on daily wage.

Monitoring by the Officials

In Tamil Nadu concerned block officials visit schools (centres) frequently. In Tamil Nadu, visit of the officials is mandatory. The district officials as well as members of state and district level committees also visit schools and report to the higher officials and concerned higher committee. In Gujarat, Deputy Mamlatdar/Deputy Tahsildar, Taluk Education Instructor, visit schools frequently whereas in Himachal Pradesh, Block Elementary Education Officer, keep in touch of the schools. Similarly, district level officers also visit schools timely.

In Andhra Pradesh, Mandal Education Officer, Mandal Resource Person, Mandal Revenue Officer, Deputy Education Officer, etc. visit schools. In Uttar Pradesh, Assistant Basic

Education Officer, Assistant Block Officer, Circle Deputy Inspector (Education), etc. visit schools. In West Bengal, Block Extension Officer, Block Relief Officer, Additional Inspector of School, etc. visit schools frequently. Apart from the above visits; the School Heads also keep vigilance on the function of the scheme. The head of the school inform to the cook for preparation of food according to attendance of day-to-day.

During visit, officials concentrate on quality and quantity of supplied food, hygienic issues, verification of stocks, utilization of convergence cost, etc. It is noticed that monitoring is a regular feature especially by the officials whereas members belonging to grassroots level committee (Gram Panchayat) were not concentrating on this aspect. This committee found inactive and moreover, it has not even constituted in State like Tamil Nadu, Andhra Pradesh, Uttar Pradesh, and West Bengal. But on the place of Mid-Day Meal Committee the Village Education Committee covers issues of mid-day meal in its agenda as part of educational development in the village. The Village Education Committee organizes its meeting regularly.

In Tamil Nadu, this scheme runs by Rural Development Department when All India Adi Dravidum Mungdam Kangdam (AIADMK) comes in power whereas Dravidum Mungdam Kangdam (DMK) give priority to Social Welfare Department for implementation of the scheme. In Gujarat, Himachal Pradesh, Andhra Pradesh and West Bengal, School Education Department functions as nodal department of the scheme whereas in Uttar Pradesh, Director Mid-day Meal Scheme has been created as nodal department for smooth function of scheme in the State.

Implementation of the Scheme at Grassroots Level

In Tamil Nadu and Gujarat, this scheme runs by the additional staff like organizer, cook supported by the helper whereas in Himachal Pradesh, one teacher from each school has been engaged under the scheme to look after works like collection of foodgrains, maintenance of records especially stock register, consumption of foodgrains day-wise, expenditure of financial assistance, preparation and submission of utilization certificate, management of gas especially when crises of supply emerges, etc. It is found that involvement of teachers especially one from each school leads problem against justification of their job charts. Under such circumstances, teachers do not able to concentrate on education and do not able to complete syllabus in time. On the other side, teachers are being used for non-academic works. In Andhra Pradesh and West Bengal, this scheme run by the members of self-help groups whereas in Uttar Pradesh, this scheme looks after by the Pradhan (Sarpanch of Gram Panchayat) with the help of cook for which Pradhan pays remuneration of Rs. 500 to cook. In Uttar Pradesh, Pradhan involves low manpower despite high enrolment of the students. This study finds that in Andhra Pradesh, one or two women especially aged of particular self-help group cook food for the students and they continue for long period. In real terms the process of cooking is not being transferred from one to other group or even within the group. All the young women prefer to work in agriculture-fields where they got opportunity for higher remuneration. Rotation among the members between one to another group or within group is low in Andhra Pradesh as compared to West Bengal. In West Bengal, four to six women involved at a time in cooking and serving process. The Government of West Bengal pays remuneration of Rs. 600 per month school-wise which shares among the involved women. This study finds that remuneration of cook is not regular in all the studied States except in Tamil Nadu.

Kitchen Sheds

In Tamil Nadu, the facility of kitchen shed was available in 19 schools whereas in Gujarat, the same was available in 11 schools. In Gujarat, the entire kitchen sheds were constructed under Tribal Sub-Plan and Swarnjayanti Gramin Rozgar Yojana (SGRY) whereas in Himachal Pradesh, not a single school was facilitated with kitchen shed. The food in general, cooks in one corner of the room where students sit. In Himachal Pradesh, most of the schools (19 out of 20) have got connection of LPG. Similarly, foodgrains also dump in corner of a room which uses for different purpose like classroom, staff room and official records. In Andhra Pradesh, the kitchen sheds were not being constructed uniformly even from one to other district. In the process of kitchen shed, Nalgonda district was lagging behind compared to Guntur and Chittoor districts. In West Bengal, a sizable number of the schools of North 24 Parganas and Burdwan have got facility of the kitchen sheds whereas in Malda district none of the school was covered under the kitchen shed. In all the six States, wherever the kitchen sheds were provided were constructed under schemes like untied funds, Jawahar Rojgar Yojana (JRY), Swarnjayanti Gramin Rozgar Yojana (SGRY), Sarva Shiksha Abhiyan (SSA), etc. In Uttar Pradesh, a sizable number of schools were not having kitchen sheds. This study finds that despite kitchen sheds, food was prepared outside in open space or in and around kitchen sheds. This practice has developed due to unhealthy construction of kitchen sheds.

This study finds that vessels provided for cooking were become old and were not suitable to use continuously. On the other side, enrolments of students increase every year but vessels are not replaced which leads problem for the cooking staff. The cook finds difficulty to boil food properly. In Tamil Nadu, the strength of students, who supposed to take food under the scheme decide well in advance or in beginning of the academic year, and accordingly food is being served throughout the year but such system is not prevalent in other States.

In Himachal Pradesh, all the sample schools do not get supply of required foodgrains in time due to non-availability of stock with the dealers. This leads problem to serve enough quantity of food to the children according to prescribed guidelines. The shortage of foodgrains compensates by the dealers in next supply but this problem affects dietary habit of the students. It has become a practice to serve low quantity of food to the students when required foodgrains is not supplied by the dealers.

Arrangement of Lunch by the Community

This study finds that in Gujarat and Himachal Pradesh, community provides lunch to the students occasionally when and then community perform ritual functions individually like marriage, birth or death anniversary, worship, etc. This system reduces burden on Government in terms of expenditure to large extent, and moreover, this system motivates society. Of course, this system is not new in society; this system has been existing from time immemorial in Indian social structure where students and families belonging to the weaker sections (social ladder) used to receive food from the higher communities on different ceremonies. This traditional system is active in Gujarat and Himachal Pradesh whereas in other studied States this system has not been activated. In sample schools of Gujarat, community supplied plates and glasses to the students in memories of their beloved who passed away. Similarly, teachers also supplies plates and glasses to the students when they take superannuation. This system has also not been observed in other studied States.

Basic Facilities in School Premises

This study finds that almost all the schools have got facility of potable water. The students of sample schools approach hand pumps, and tap water which are accessible in the school premises. In areas studied it is found that all the sample schools have got connection of electricity except schools located in Nalgonda district of Andhra Pradesh. In few schools, lavatories were common especially for female teachers and for the girl students. In some of the schools lavatories were provided to the teachers both male and female including girls whereas boys were not allowed to use such lavatories due to scarcity of water which lead to bad smell. The facility of lavatories is not uniformly provided from one to other State. During these days, the basic facilities both teaching and non-teaching provide under Sarva Shiksha Abhiyan (SSA) which fulfil basic requirements like teacher grant, building grant, repairing grants, etc.

Flow of Fund and Reply of Utilization

The Government of India makes allotment of financial assistance through the State Governments twice in a year. The State Government transfers funds to the districts based on strength of students. Each district relocates funds to the schools through mandal office (in Andhra Pradesh), taluk office (in Gujarat) or block office. The requirements of assistance calculate based on strength of students in the beginning of the academic year. The responsibility of utilization of funds need to submit from school to block, block to district, district to State and State to Government of India. In case of Andhra Pradesh and Gujarat, the same has been routed through the mandal office and taluk office. In case, number of students increase then prior permission need to take from concerned authority of mandal, block and taluk officers. This study finds that concerned official do not furnish relevant information including utilization certificate which leads problem by the Government of India to release next instalment in time.

Quality of Education

This study finds that mid-day meal scheme shows school to the children everyday or in other words, enrolment of the children has improved because of the schemes but quality of education especially at elementary stage is loosing its grip because of various reasons like; engagement of teachers in non-academic works, lack of proper trained teachers, apathetic attitude of the teachers, non-recruitment of teachers for longer, lack of proper infrastructure in schools in terms of enough rooms and moreover, whatever rooms are available used for store and record purpose and apart from this, teachers make ups and down especially those who belong to urban and semi-urban areas, indiscipline among the teachers, lack of community cooperation, promotion of students in higher class without developing basic learning, etc. creates barriers against the healthy education.

This study finds that majority of the students who were studying in fourth or even in fifth class were not able to read moderately text-books which promulgated by the State Governments. This situation found in most of the schools of all the six States. Supply of food is priority of the concern but quality of education should not be ignored simultaneously, therefore, both should be run together without distributing to each other. The qualified, disciplined and dedicated teachers required for promoting education. In sample schools, vidhya volunteers belonging to the same village or adjoining villages were posted on low remuneration whereas the priority need to give those youths who had already obtained qualification and training of teaching. This problem can be sorted out by recruiting timely trained teachers. Similarly, the objective of the scheme is not merely feed the children whose parents are unable to feed them but need to prove expectation of the society and state which quote that children are future of the country.

Recommendations

- This study strongly recommends that community participation is essential to make the scheme healthy. This will help on many issues like replacement of vessels, mat and sort out problem of safe drinking water; make appeal for gas connection, healthcare of the children, maintenance of healthy environment in the school premises, supply of food on social occasions, etc. including boosting enrolment of the children,
- The Mid-Day Meal Scheme Committee (MDMSC) should be merged in Village Education Committee (VEC) because Village Education Committee is broad and moreover, it organizes meeting regularly. The merging process will save time of the concerned members and however, most of the members like Sarpanchs/Pradhan, Parents, and School Heads represent both the committees,
- To save further degradation of forest or vegetations, all the Mid-Day Meal Schools need to connect with solar cooking system or to ensure supply of gas in time,

- Each school should have specious kitchen shed consisting of proper ventilations, light, proper height, and with store facility. The kitchen shed need to locate little away from the classrooms. This will make students to concentrate on education rather than watching kitchen.
- The teachers especially in Himachal Pradesh need to be exempted from the assigned task. In Himachal Pradesh, the post of organizer, cook and helper need to create like available in Tamil Nadu and Gujarat so teachers can pay attention on education. Their involvement certainly degrades education.
- This scheme could be run through the women belonging to self-help group who are efficient in maintaining of the accounts. In this regard, women who obtained primary or upper primary education should be given preference. Such women are now available within the village or adjoining villages.
- The essential commodities such as edible oil, condiments, salt, gas, etc. should be supplied along with foodgrains to the schools like Government of Tamil Nadu has been supplying. This process saves transportation cost and manpower.
- The foodgrains need to supply based on local requirements. Local cereals could be procured in godowns. In famine, such compulsion need to be exempted and flexibility should be given to supply of the non-local foodgrains.
- Parents need to make educate and responsible for promoting education of their children. To stop their migration, employment opportunities need to promote in rural areas. This will reduce child labour system. Mahatma Gandhi National Rural Employment Guarantee Scheme (MGNREGS) is a right step on this issue but there is a need to boost self-employment rather than depending on wage employment,
- Food should be served in time so that study could run smoothly. Students especially those who take food at

home and come back to the school in time bound to wait for further session because of the flexibility in lunch hours. This affects to such students who are really keen on study.

REFERENCES

Agrawal, S.P. and Agrawal, J.C. (1997) "Development of Education in India", Concept Publishing Company Pvt. Ltd., New Delhi

Nutritional Support to Education Report of the Committee on Mid-day Meals (1995) Annexure: Guidelines for a Scheme of Central Assistance for Provision of Mid-Day Meals to Children in Primary Schools in the Country during the Seventh Plan, (May 1995).

National Programme of Nutritional Support to Primary Education, (2004) 'Guidelines' Ministry of Human Resource Development (Department of Elementary Education and Literacy), Government of India.

National Programme of Nutritional Support to Primary Education, (2006) 'Revised Guidelines' Ministry of Human Resource Development (Department of Elementary Education and Literacy), Government of India.

"Policy Note" (2004-05) School Education Department, Ministry for Education and Backward Classes, Government of Tamil Nadu.

"Educational Statistics" (2005-06) Sarva Shiksha Abhiyan, Himachal Pradesh, DPEP Bhavan, Lalpani, Shimla.

Sikligar, P.C. "Operation Blackboard: Attitudes and Approaches", *Economic Studies*, Vol. 32, No. 2, November, 1993.

Annexure

Mid-Day Meal Scheme
Central Assistance Admissible to States/UTs during 2008-09 (As on 17.6.08)

Sl. No.	State/UT	Primary							Upper-Primary						Total (Pry.+Up. Pry.)	Released as first instalment (25%). (Pry. + Up. Pry.)
		No. of children to to be covered	No. of Working Days for Pry. & Up. Pry.	Central Assistance Admissible: Cooking Cost	Central Assistance Admissible: Trans-portation Cost	Central Assistance Admissible: MME	Total Primary	Released as first instalment (25% of Col. 8)	No. of children to be covered	Central Assistance Admissible: Cooking Cost	Central Assistance Admissible: Trans-portation Cost	Central Assistance Admissible: MME	Total (Up. Pry)	Released as first Instalment (25% of Col. 4)		
1	2	3	4	5	6	7	8	9	10	11	12	13	14	15	16	17
Non-NER States																
1.	Andhra Pradesh	5073213	220	17634.48	837.08	442.98	18914.54	4728.63	1814065	8380.98	448.98	218.20	9048.16	2262.03	27962.70	6990.66
2.	Bihar	6879084	217	23585.62	1119.57	592.47	25297.66	6324.40	2679121	12208.75	654.04	317.86	13180.65	3295.15	38478.31	9619.55
3.	Chhattisgarh	2208519	206	7188.28	341.21	180.57	7710.06	1927.51	1095754	4740.23	253.94	123.41	5117.58	1279.38	12827.64	3206.89
4.	Goa	76240	210	252.96	12.00	6.35	271.31	67.82	59460	262.21	14.04	6.82	283.07	70.76	554.38	138.58
5.	Gujarat	3263166	214	11033.41	523.73	277.16	11834.30	2958.57	885301	3978.54	213.13	103.58	4295.25	1073.80	16129.55	4032.37
6.	Haryana	1300997	204	4193.37	199.05	105.33	4497.75	1124.43	605693	2594.78	139.00	67.55	2801.33	700.32	7299.08	1824.75
7.	Himachal Pradesh	500983	232	1836.40	145.28	47.17	2028.85	507.21	350874	1709.45	152.63	45.60	1907.68	476.92	3936.53	984.13
8.	Jammu & Kashmir	962747	208	3163.97	250.31	81.28	3495.56	873.88	281567	1229.88	109.81	32.81	1372.50	343.12	4868.06	1217.00
9.	Jharkhand	2842880	229	10286.10	488.26	258.38	11032.74	2758.17	827236	3978.17	213.11	103.57	4294.85	1073.70	15327.59	3831.87
10.	Karnataka	3779006	212	12658.15	600.86	317.97	13576.98	3394.23	2031143	9042.64	484.42	235.43	9762.49	2440.61	23339.47	5834.84
11.	Kerala	1909491	200	6033.99	286.42	151.57	6471.98	1617.98	1327695	5576.31	298.73	145.18	6020.22	1505.04	12492.20	3123.02
12.	Madhya Pradesh	6702631	219	23192.44	1100.90	582.59	24875.93	6218.97	2107977	9694.58	519.35	252.40	10466.33	2616.57	35342.26	8835.54
13.	Maharashtra	8132481	220	28268.50	1341.85	710.11	30320.46	7580.10	3964879	18317.74	981.30	476.91	19775.95	4943.97	50096.41	12524.07
14.	Orissa	3282700	210	10891.99	517.02	273.60	11682.61	2920.64	1128000	4974.48	266.49	129.51	5370.48	1342.61	17053.09	4263.25
15.	*Punjab	1300279	220	4519.76	214.54	113.53	4847.83	1211.95	868849	4014.08	215.04	104.50	4333.62	1083.40	9181.45	2295.35
16.	Rajasthan	4131581	200	13055.79	619.73	327.96	14003.48	3500.86	1770400	7435.68	398.34	193.59	8027.61	2006.89	22031.09	5507.75
17.	Tamil Nadu	3531891	214	11942.02	566.86	299.98	12808.86	3202.20	1831070	8075.01	432.59	210.23	8717.83	2179.44	21526.69	5381.64
18.	Uttarakhand	731105	203	2344.94	185.51	60.24	2590.69	647.66	393444	1677.25	149.75	44.74	1871.74	467.92	4462.43	1115.58
19.	Uttar Pradesh	13760021	205	44568.70	2115.60	1119.57	47803.87	11950.96	4173094	17965.16	962.41	467.73	19395.30	4848.82	67199.17	16799.78
20.	West Bengal	7133880	210	23670.21	1123.58	594.60	25388.39	6347.09	3816192	16829.40	901.57	438.16	18169.13	4542.28	43557.52	10889.37
	Total	**77502895**		**260321.08**	**12589.36**	**6543.41**	**279453.85**	**69863.26**	**32011814**	**142685.32**	**7808.6/**	**3717.78**	**154211.77**	**38552.73**	**433665.62**	**108415.99**

(Contd.)

Annexure *(Contd.)*

Sl. No.	State/UT	Primary: No. of children to be covered	Primary: No. of Working Days for Pry. & Up. Pry.	Primary: Central Assistance Admissible: Cooking Cost	Primary: Central Assistance Admissible: Trans-portation Cost	Primary: Central Assistance Admissible: MME	Total Primary	Released as first instalment (25% of Col. 8)	Upper-Primary: No. of children to be covered	Upper-Primary: Central Assistance Admissible: Cooking Cost	Upper-Primary: Central Assistance Admissible: Trans-portation Cost	Upper-Primary: Central Assistance Admissible: MME	Total (Up. Pry)	Released as first Instalment (25% of Col. 4)	Total (Pry.+Up. Pry.)	Released as first instalment (25%). (Pry. + Up. Pry.)
1	2	3	4	5	6	7	8	9	10	11	12	13	14	15	16	17
UTs with Legislature																
21.	Delhi	986067	200	3115.97	147.91	78.27	3342.15	835.52	535895	2250.75	120.57	58.59	2429.91	607.46	5772.06	1442.98
22.	Pondicherry	54540	200		172.34818	4.32	184.84	46.20	40488	170.04	9.10	4.42	183.56	45.88	368.40	92.08
	Total	**1040607**		**3288.31**	**156.09**	**82.59**	**3526.99**	**881.72**	**576383**	**2420.79**	**129.67**	**63.01**	**2613**	**653.34**	**6140.46**	**1535.06**
UTs without Legislature																
23.	Andaman & Nicobar Islands	23661	207	77.38	3.67	1.94	82.99	20.73	15719	68.33	3.66	1.77	73.76	18.43	156.75	39.16
24.	Chandigarh	53163	210	176.39	8.37	4.43	189.19	47.28	32000	141.12	7.56	3.67	152.35	38.08	341.54	85.36
25	Dadar &Nagar Haveli	30000	216	102.38	4.86	2.57	109.81	27.44	8500	38.55	2.06	1.00	41.61	10.39	151.42	37.83
26.	Daman & Diu	13346	209	44.07	2.09	1.10	47.26	11.80	5134	22.53	1.20	0.58	24.31	6.07	71.57	17.87
27.	Lakshadweep	7094	220	24.65	1.17	3.27	29.09		2562	11.83	0.63	0.30	12.76		41.85	0.00
	Total	**127264**		**424.87**	**20.16**	**13.31**	**458.34**	**107.55**	**63915**	**282.36**	**15.11**	**7.32**	**306**	**72.97**	**763.13**	**180.22**
NER STATES																
28.	Arunachal Pradesh	120699	200	456.24	30.17	11.14	497.55	128.38	60650	292.94	22.74	7.48	323.16	80.78	820.71	205.16
29.	Assam	2427900	206	9452.78	625.18	230.91	10308.87	2577.21	1835693	9132.38	709.03	233.30	10074.71	2518.66	20383.58	5095.87
30.	Manipur	234386	210	930.27	61.52	22.72	1014.51	253.63	66080	335.12	26.01	8.56	369.69	92.42	1384.20	346.05
31.	Meghalaya	260116	200	983.23	65.02	24.01	1072.26	268.06	139859	675.51	52.44	17.25	745.20	186.30	1817.46	454.36
32.	Mizoram	89709	205	347.57	22.98	8.49	379.04	94.75	62562	309.72	24.04	7.91	341.67	85.41	720.71	180.16
33.	Nagaland	180854	200	683.62	45.21	16.69	745.52	186.37	34039	164.40	12.76	4.20	181.36	45.34	926.88	231.71
34.	Sikkim	57637	200	217.86	14.40	5.32	237.58	59.39	28693	138.58	10.76	3.54	152.88	38.21	390.46	97.60
35.	Tripura	348020	220	1447.06	95.70	35.34	1578.10	394.51	163299	867.60	67.36	22.16	957.12	239.28	2535.22	633.79
	Total	**3719321**		**14518.63**	**960.18**	**354.62**	**15833.43**	**3958.30**	**2390875**	**11916.25**	**925.14**	**304.40**	**13145.79**	**3286.40**	**28979.22**	**7244.70**
	GRAND TOTAL	**82390087**		**278552.89**	**13725.79**	**6993.93**	**299272.61**	**74810.53**	**35042987**	**157304.72**	**8878.59**	**4092.51**	**170275.82**	**42565.44**	**469548.43**	**117375.97**
	GRAND TOTAL IN CRORES			**2785.53**	**137.26**	**69.94**	**2992.73**	**748.11**		**1573.05**	**88.79**	**40.93**	**1702.76**	**425.65**	**4695.48**	**1173.76**

* No. of working days for Up. Pry. Stage—210 days.

Grand Total (Pry. + Up. Pry.)—4695.48 crore.

APPENDIX

The Human Right to Food in India

George Kent
University of Hawai'i
April 18, 2002

The website of the Indian Embassy in Washington, D.C. offers an account of "Agriculture and Rural Developments" in India. Its first paragraph describes "A Saga of Success":

From a nation dependent on food imports to feed its population, India today is not only self-sufficient in grain production, but also has a substantial reserve. The progress made by agriculture in the last four decades has been one of the biggest success stories of free India. Agriculture and allied activities constitute the single largest contributor to the Gross Domestic Product, almost 33 per cent of it. Agriculture is the means of livelihood of about two-thirds of the workforce in the country.

It is true that the country now produces enough food to feed all of its people. India no longer suffers through large-scale famines as it has in the past. When there are rapid increases in hunger in some parts of India, it is now usually attributed to short-term natural events such as hurricanes or droughts. These are described as transitory, episodic events, temporary deviations from normal.

However, this upbeat version of the food situation in India neglects the reality of widespread chronic malnutrition in the country. Temporary disruptions in the food system by natural calamities are disastrous for so many people only because they live so close to the edge of disaster under normal conditions. India could feed all of its people, but it doesn't. The chronic conditions—the conditions that are normal—for many millions of people in India are unacceptable in terms of the basic requirements of human dignity.

The problems are not rooted in the vagaries of natural phenomena, but in deeply embedded political and economic patterns. There are massive Governmental programmes—or "schemes" as they are called—for feeding poor children, providing subsidized foods, etc.—but still the problems persist. Enormous amounts of money are spent on such programmes. Yet, somehow, the benefits don't reach the people who need them most.

There is a story now unfolding that helps us to understand how things can go so wrong. The Central Government of India has been storing many millions of tonnes of grain while people are starving. That is not new. What is new is that a human rights organization in India, the People's Union of Civil Liberties (PUCL), has challenged this practice in the Supreme Court of India. Light is being shined into places that had been well hidden, and the scandal is being thoroughly aired in India's media.

The case is being tried on the basis of India's Constitution and its federal and state laws, especially its famed *Famine Code*. This review shows how the case fits into the framework of international human rights, and specifically the human right to adequate food. Viewing the case in this larger context, we can see that this case is relevant to food assistance programmes in every country, and to international humanitarian assistance as well.

THE SUPREME COURT CASE

On April 16, 2001, the PUCL submitted a "writ petition" to the Supreme Court of India asking three major questions:

A. Starvation death is a natural phenomenon while there is a surplus stock of foodgrains in the Government godown. Does the right to life mean that people who are starving and who are too poor to buy foodgrains ought to be given foodgrains free of cost by the State from the surplus stock lying with the State, particularly when it is reported that a large part of it is lying unused and rotting?

B. Does not the right to life under Article 21 of the Constitution of India include the right to food?

C. Does not the right to food, which has been upheld by the Hon'ble Court, imply that the State has a duty to provide food especially in situations of drought, to people who are drought affected and are not in a position to purchase food?

Article 21 of the Constitution, entitled "Protection of life and personal liberty", says, in its entirety, "No person shall be deprived of his life or personal liberty except according to procedure established by law."

As a result of the ongoing proceedings, the Supreme Court has been issuing orders calling upon Government agencies to identify the needy within their jurisdictions, and to ensure that they receive adequate food. For example, on July 23, 2001, the court said:

In our opinion, what is of utmost importance is to see that food is provided to the aged, infirm, disabled, destitute women, destitute men who are in danger of starvation, pregnant and lactating women and destitute children, especially in cases where they or members of their family do not have sufficient funds to provide food for them. In case of famine, there may be shortage of food, but here the situation is that amongst plenty there is scarcity. Plenty of food is available, but distribution of the same amongst the very poor and the destitute is scarce and non-existent leading to mal-nourishment, starvation and other related problems.

On September 3, 2001, the court directed that 16 states and Union Territories that had not identified families below the poverty line must do so within two weeks, so that those families could be provided with food assistance. After two weeks, on September 17, 2001, the court reprimanded them, saying, "we are not satisfied that any such exercise in the right earnestness has been undertaken." They were then given another three weeks to comply with the order. The court also reminded the states that "certain schemes of the Central Government are mentioned which are required to be implemented by State Governments":

These schemes are: Employment Assurance Scheme which may have been replaced by a Sampurna Gramin Yojana, Mid-day Meal Scheme, Integrated Child Development Scheme, National Benefit Maternity Scheme for BPL pregnant women, National Old Age Pension Scheme for destitute persons of over 65 years, Annapurna Scheme, Antyodaya Anna Yojana, National Family Benefit Scheme and Public Distribution Scheme for BPL and APL families. The Chief Secretaries of all the States and the Union Territories are hereby directed to report to the Cabinet Secretary, with copy to the learned Attorney General, within three weeks from today with regard to the implementation of all or any of these Schemes with or without any modification and if all or any of the Schemes have not been implemented then the reasons for the same.

All State Governments were directed to take their "entire allotment of foodgrains from the Central Government under the various Schemes and disburse the same in accordance with the Schemes". Further, the court required that "the Food for Work Programme in the scarcity areas should also be implemented by the various States to the extent possible".

On November 28, 2001, the court issued directions to eight of the major schemes, calling on them to identify the needy and to provide them with grain and other services by early 2002. For example, for the Targeted Public Distribution Scheme, "The States are directed to complete the identification of BPL (below poverty level) families, issuing of cards, and commencement of distribution of 25 kgs. grain per family per month latest by 1st January, 2002."

THE RIGHT TO FOOD INTERNATIONALLY

The orders issued by the court clearly established that the court understands the right to life, affirmed in article 21 of India's Constitution, as implying the right to food. While the court has been guided entirely by national law, it could also draw on recent advances made in understanding the right to food at the global level.

There is increasing recognition worldwide of the human right to adequate food. There is a legal obligation to assure that all people are adequately nourished. The articulation of the human right to adequate food in modern international human rights law arises in the context of the broader human right to an adequate standard of living. The *Universal Declaration of Human Rights* of 1948 asserts in Article 25(1) that "everyone has the right to a standard of living adequate for the health and well-being of himself and his family, including food".

The human right to adequate food was subsequently reaffirmed in two major binding international agreements. In the *International Covenant on Economic, Social and Cultural Rights* (which came into force in 1976), Article 11 says that "The States Parties to the present Covenant recognize the right of everyone to an adequate standard of living for himself and his family, including adequate food, clothing, and housing" and also recognizes "the fundamental right of everyone to be free from hunger ".

In the *Convention on the Rights of the Child* (which came into force in 1990), two articles address the issue of nutrition. Article 24 says that "States Parties recognize the right of the child to the enjoyment of the highest attainable standard of health (paragraph 1)" and shall take appropriate measures "to combat disease and malnutrition through the provision of adequate nutritious foods, clean drinking water, and health-care (paragraph 2c)." Article 24 also says that States Parties shall take appropriate measures "To ensure that all segments of society, in particular parents and children, are informed, have access to education and are supported in the use of basic knowledge of child health and nutrition [and] the advantages of breastfeeding". Article 27 says in paragraph 3 that States Parties "shall in case of need provide material assistance and support programmes, particularly with regard to nutrition, clothing, and housing".

Even if the human right to adequate food had not been stated directly, it would be strongly implied in other provisions such as those asserting the right to life and health, or the *Convention on the Rights of the Child*'s requirement (in article 24, paragraph 2a) that States Parties shall "take appropriate measures to diminish infant and child mortality". The human right to adequate food has been reaffirmed at the international level in many different settings.

Beginning in the late 1990s, work on the human right to adequate food at the global level centred on a mandate from the World Food Summit held in Rome in 1996. In the Summit's concluding *Plan of Action,* Objective 7.4 called upon the UN High Commissioner for Human Rights, in consultation with relevant treaty bodies, and in collaboration with relevant specialized agencies and programmes of the UN system and appropriate inter-Governmental mechanisms, to better define the rights related to food in Article 11 of the Covenant and to propose ways to implement and realize these rights.

A series of expert consultations, conferences, and studies steadily clarified the meaning of the human right to food. This effort culminated with the publication on May 12, 1999 by the UN's Committee on Economic, Social and Cultural Rights of its *General Comment 12 (Twentieth Session, 1999): The Right to Adequate Food (Art. 11).* This statement by the committee constitutes a definitive contribution to international jurisprudence.

Paragraph 5 of *General Comment 12* observes, "Fundamentally, the roots of the problem of hunger and malnutrition are not lack of food but lack of *access to* available food, *inter alia* because of poverty, by large segments of the world's population." The reference here is to the fundamental distinction between *availability* (is there food around?) and *access* (can you make a claim on that food?). Paragraph 6 presents the core definition:

The right to adequate food is realized when every man, woman and child, alone or in community with others, has physical and economic access at all times to adequate food or means for its procurement.

General Comment 12 paragraph 7 explains that *adequacy* means that account must be taken of what is appropriate under given circumstances. Food *security* implies food being accessible for both present and future generations. *Sustainability* relates to long-term availability and accessibility. Thus, as explained in paragraph 8, the core content of the right to adequate food implies:

The availability of food in a quantity and quality sufficient to satisfy the dietary needs of individuals, free from adverse substances, and acceptable within a given culture.

The accessibility of such food in ways that are sustainable and that do not interfere with the enjoyment of other human rights. Paragraph 14 summarizes the obligations of States as follows:

Every State is obliged to ensure for everyone under its jurisdiction access to the minimum essential food which is sufficient, nutritionally adequate and safe, to ensure their freedom from hunger.

Paragraph 15 draws out the different kinds or levels of obligations of the state. These obligations may be sorted into categories as follows:

- *respect*—"The obligation to *respect* existing access to adequate food requires States parties not to take any measures that result in preventing such access."
- *protect*—"The obligation to *protect* requires measures by the State to ensure that enterprises or individuals do not deprive individuals of their access to adequate food."
- *fulfil (facilitate)*—"The obligation to *fulfil (facilitate)* means the State must proactively engage in activities intended to strengthen people's access to and utilization of resources and means to ensure their livelihood, including food security."
- *fulfil (provide)*—"Finally, whenever an individual or group is unable, for reasons beyond their control, to enjoy the right to adequate food by the means at their disposal, States have the obligation to *fulfil (provide)* that

> right directly. This obligation also applies for persons who are victims of natural or other disasters."

General Comment 12 also addresses the issues of implementation at the national level, framework legislation, monitoring, remedies and accountability, and international obligations.

The primary responsibility of National Governments is to *facilitate*, which means assuring that there are *enabling conditions* that allow people to provide for themselves. However, where people are not able to feed themselves adequately, Governments have some obligation to provide for them. While international law does not specify the character or level of assistance that is required, it is clear that, at the very least; people must not be allowed to go hungry. Article 11 of the *International Covenant on Economic, Social and Cultural Rights* recognizes "the fundamental right of everyone to be free from hunger". Paragraph 6 of *General Comment 12* explains, "States have a core obligation to take the necessary action to mitigate and alleviate hunger as provided for in paragraph 2 of Article 11, even in times of natural or other disasters." Paragraph 14 adds, "Every State is obliged to ensure for everyone under its jurisdiction access to the minimum essential food which is sufficient, nutritionally adequate and safe, to ensure their freedom from hunger." Paragraph 17 says, "Violations of the Covenant occur when a State fails to ensure the satisfaction of, at the very least, the minimum essential level required to be free from hunger." There is no ambiguity here.

STARVATION IS NOT THE PROBLEM

To repeat the main definition:

The right to adequate food is realized when every man, woman and child, alone or in community with others, has physical and economic access at all times to adequate food or means for its procurement.

It is clear that this goal has not been achieved in India. Perhaps even more important, at this stage, is the fact that the realization of the right to food has not been clearly established as the Government's goal.

Much of the debate in India has centred on the question of whether there have in fact been large numbers of starvation deaths. Those who say no, and thus defend the Government, take a narrow view of the meaning of "starvation". They take it to mean deaths directly attributable to an extreme lack of food, and they focus on adult deaths. In fact, most deaths associated with malnutrition are due to a combination of malnutrition and disease. The immediate, final cause of death, the phrase written on the death certificate, is usually some disease, often an infectious disease, rather than starvation or hunger as such. UNICEF estimates that in the year 2000, about 2,420,000 children in India died before their fifth birthdays. This was the highest total for any country. It was estimated that for the same year about 10,929,000 children died before their fifth birthdays. Thus, more than a fifth of the child mortality worldwide occurs in India alone. The international agencies estimate that about half of these deaths of children under five are associated with malnutrition. Thus we can estimate that more than a million children die in India each year from causes associated with malnutrition. To that number must be added a large but unknown number of adults who succumb for the same reason.

In their data keeping, international agencies such as the United Nations Children's Fund and the World Health Organization do not keep records on starvation deaths. No one does. Even in the worst of times, few people die immediately and directly from starvation. They die more slowly, from malnutrition in combination with disease. Yes, if one takes a narrow view of the meaning of starvation, there are few starvation deaths in India. But using this trick of language to suggest that there is no serious problem of malnutrition in a country like India borders on the criminal.

India's Government agencies at both Central and State levels seem to have trouble seeing the massive hunger that characterizes India. This is apparent in the working agenda of the National Institute of Nutrition in Hyderabad. The institute occupies itself with minor technical questions, and does experimental studies on questions that can be addressed quite adequately in developed countries, while practically ignoring the deep and widespread hunger all around the country. Technical research avoids facing up to the problem, which is deeply political. There is no hope of solving the hunger problem if the Government and its agencies refuse to see it.

In developed countries, hunger may be hard to see, but in developing countries, the suggestion that there is no hunger can only be a matter of deliberate denial. Some in Government in India are suggesting that the poor have no serious problems, while many of the poor are in such deep despair that they are committing suicide.

THE MISSING PIECE IN INDIA'S RIGHTS SYSTEM

As a party to the *International Covenant on Economic, Social and Cultural Rights* and the *Convention on the Rights of the Child*, India has committed itself to honouring the right to adequate food. Moreover, in response to a question raised in Parliament regarding the status of children's nutrition rights, the Department of Women and Child Development answered as follows, on December 7, 1993 in the Lok Sabha and December 10, 1993 in the Rajya Sabha:

The Government of India has ratified the UN Convention on the Rights of the Child. Appropriate legislative and administrative measures are being taken for implementing the Convention by the concerned Ministries/Departments.

A National Plan of Action on Children has been adopted under which goals have been fixed for the decade 1990-2000. The Plan seeks to cover the programmes in the areas of Child and Maternal Health, Nutrition, Water and Sanitation, Education, Children in difficult circumstances and adolescent girls. All sectors have reviewed their programmes for strengthening keeping in view the goals set in National Plan of Action on Children.

A number of child care programmes for improving the nutritional status of children are being implemented. Integrated

Child Development Service (ICDS) Programme is a major intervention for providing a package of services including supplementary nutrition to 1.63 crore children under 6 years of age. Nutrition supplementation is also being provided to children under the scheme of creches (3 lakh children) and Balwadi Nutrition (2.29 lakh children). A new initiative to improve nutritional status of adolescent girls has been started, on a selected basis, in 507 ICDS Projects. Again, through nutrition education programmes the mothers are also being educated and empowered to look after the nutritional needs of their children better.

While the reply offered in the Parliament discussed the situation with regard to food-related *programmes,* more is needed to fully address the question of the *right* to food. What is that right, and where is it elaborated in the law? Whose right is it? To what extent is this right implemented? And what are the mechanisms of accountability for assuring that the right is realized?

In any rights system there are three distinct roles to be fulfilled: the *rights holders,* the *duty bearers,* and the *agents of accountability.* The task of the agents of accountability is to make sure that those who have the duty to carry out their obligations to those who have the rights.

To describe a rights system, we need to know the identities and also the functions of those who carry out these roles. We would also want to know the mechanisms or structures through which these functions are to be carried out. Thus, we would want to know:

A. The nature of the *rights holders* and their rights;
B. The nature of the duty-bearers and their obligations corresponding to the rights of the rights holders; and
C. The nature of the agents of accountability, and the procedures through which they assure that the duty bearers meet their obligations to the rights holders. The accountability mechanisms include, in particular, the remedies available to the rights holders themselves.

These are the three core components, the "ABCs" of rights systems. A rights system can be understood as a kind of cybernetic self-regulating arrangement designed to assure that rights are realized. In any cybernetic system, a goal is decided upon, and means are established for reaching that goal. In addition, there are specific means for making corrections in case there are deviations from the path towards the goal. This is the self-regulating aspect of the system. With regard to the human right to adequate food, the goal is to end hunger and malnutrition.

Any Government can say it has such lofty goals. These things may even be promised in the Nation's Constitution. But we know that there are many cases in which Governments go off course and fail to deliver on their promises. In nations where there is an effective rights system, however, there are specific mechanisms for calling the Government to account; that is, for making course corrections. The most fundamental of these mechanisms of accountability is for rights holders themselves to have effective remedies through which they can complain and have the Government's behaviour corrected. This is the missing piece in India's system for addressing the right to food. Where there are no effective remedies, there are no effective rights.

Intervention by the Supreme Court is a mechanism of accountability, but it is not normally available to ordinary people on a local basis. The present Supreme Court case in India has become necessary because there are no effective mechanisms of accountability available to ordinary people at the local level. Until local people know their rights and know that they have effective means through which to exercise them, there is no effective system for assuring the realization of the right to adequate food in India.

Bibliography

Note: A website on the grain storage case before the Supreme Court of India is being developed, at http://geocities.com/righttofood/introcase.htm

Bhatia, Bela, "In Pursuit of Relief: The Drought-Affected in Rajasthan Demand Means of Sustenance", *Frontline*, Vol. 18, No. 16 (Aug. 4-17, 2001). http://www.flonnet.com/fl1816/18160420.htm

Chhibbar, Y. P., "PUCL Petitions Supreme Court on Starvation Deaths", *PUCL Bulletin*, July 2001. http://www.pucl.org/reports/Rajasthan/2001/starvation_death.htm

Claeson, Mariam; Bos, Eduard R.; Mawji, Tazim; and Pathmanathan, Indra, "Reducing Child Mortality in India in the New Millenium," *Bulletin of the World Health Organization*, Vol. 78, No. 10 (2000), pp. 1192-1199. http://www.who.int/bulletin/pdf/2000/issue10/bu0788.pdf

Devraj, Rani, "India: Farmers Protest Against Globalization", *Third World Network*, January 25, 2001. http://www.twnside.org.sg/title/protest.htm

Devraj, Ranjit, "Indian Surpluses Go Against the Grain", *Asia Times*, September 6, 2001.

Dreze, Jean, "Right to Food and Public Accountability", *The Hindu*, December 5, 2001.

Dreze, Jean, "Starving the Poor—I", *The Hindu*, February 26, 2001. http://www.hinduonnet.com/thehindu/2001/02/26/stories/05262524.htm

Dreze, Jean, "Starving the Poor—II", *The Hindu*, February 27, 2001. http://www.hindu.com/2001/02/27/stories/05272524.htm

Embassy of India, *Agriculture and Rural Developments*. http://www.indianembassy.org/dydemo/agriculture.htm

"Ensure Jobs, Food for the Poor, SC Directs States", *Times of India*. March 4, 2002. http://timesofindia.indiatimes.com/articleshow.asp?art_id=2796496&sType=1

FAS Online, *India Fails to Reconcile Mountains of Rice with Starving People*, Foreign Agricultural Service, United States Department of Agriculture, November 9, 2001. http://www.fas.usda.gov/grain/circular/2001/10-01/article.htm

International Covenant on Economic, Social and Cultural Rights. http://www.unhchr.ch/html/menu3/b/a_cescr.htm

Kaur, Naunidhi, "Welfare Claims", *Frontline*, Vol. 18, No. 24 (Nov. 24-Dec. 7, 2001). http://www.flonnet.com/fl1824/18240570.htm

Kumar, Palash, "High Court Chastises Government as Millions of Indians Go Hungry", *PUCL (AFP)*, August 21, 2001. http://www.pucl.org/reports/Rajasthan/2001/palash.htm

Measham, Anthony and Chatterjee, Meera, *Wasting Away: The Crisis of Malnutrition in India* (Washington, D.C.: World Bank, 1999.

Menon, Parvathi, "A Farm Crisis and Suicides", *Frontline*, Vol. 18, No. 8 (Apr. 14-27, 2001). http://www.flonnet.com/fl1808/18080210.htm

Mishra, Neelabh, "Drought and Deaths", *Frontline*, Vol. 18, No. 8 (Apr. 14-27, 2001). http://www.flonnet.com/fl1808/18080710.htm

Muralidharan, Sukumar, "Upholding the Right to Food", *Frontline*, Vol. 18, No. 18 (Sep. 1-14, 2001). http://www.flonnet.com/fl1818/18181220.htm

Nandy, Pritish, "F is a Dirty Word", *Rediff.com*, May 23, 2001. http://www.rediff.com/news/2001/may/23nandy.htm

Padmanabhan, Chitra, "Starving in the Midst of Plenty", *Pitara.com*, May 19, 2001. http://www.pitara.com/news/news_india/online.asp?story=170

"Rajasthan PUCL Writ in Supreme Court on Famine Deaths", *PUCL Bulletin*, November 2001. http://www.pucl.org/reports/Rajasthan/2001/starvation-writ.htm

Reddy, C. Rammanohar, "Whatever Happened to the Sixty Million Tonnes?" The Hindu, October 28, 2001. http://www.hinduonnet.com/thehindu/mag/2001/10/28/stories/2001102800480301.htm

Sainath, P., "Rajasthan's Drought: Abundance of Food, Scarcity of Vision", *The Hindu*, March 18, 2001. http://www.hinduonnet.com/thehindu/2001/03/18/stories/13180611.htm

Saxena, Rashmi and Tiwari, Deepak, "Wolf at the Door", *The Week*, March 8, 1998. http://www.the-week.com/98mar08/events1.htm

"SC Asks Six States to End Starvation Amidst Plenty", *The Times of India*, March 12, 2002. http://timesofindia.indiatimes.com/articleshow.asp?catkey=-2128839596&art_id=1665936272&sType=1

"SC Notice to Govts on Starvation Deaths", *Times of India*, May 10, 2001.

Sharma, Devinder, "Supreme Court's Directive to Feed the Hungry", Tehelka.com, March 11, 2002. http://www.tehelka.com/channels/commentary/2001/july/27/com072701supremecourt.htm

Sharma, Devinder, "Surplus Food for Export, and . . . Animal Feed for the Hungry", *Focus*, Vol. 60 (Winter 1999/2000).

Shiva, Vandana, "At the Mercy of Globalization", *The Hindu*, September 23, 2001. http://www.hinduonnet.com/thehindu/2001/09/23/stories/13230614.htm

Singh, D.K., "Rajasthan Flounders in the Name Game: Is it Famine or Drought", Hindustantimes.com, May 6, 2001. http://www.hindustantimes.com/nonfram/070501/detNAT10.asp

Singh, Tavleen, "Grain of Untruth", *India Today*, May 28, 2001.

Slater, Joanna, "The Problem of Plenty", *Far Eastern Economic Review*, December 6, 2001.

"Starvation Looms in India's Drought-Hit Orissa State", CNN.com, December 15, 2000. http://europe.cnn.com/2000/ASIANOW/south/12/15/india.starvation.reut/

"Starvation Rears its Head in Eastern India", *The Times of India*, March 12, 2002. http://timesofindia.indiatimes.com/articleshow.asp?art_id=1481397706

Swaminathan, Srilata, "The Question of Food Security", *Commentary*. October 2001. http://www.cpiml.org/pgs/partorg/liberati/2001oct/food_sec.htm

Times of India News Service, "Supreme Court of India Asks Six States to End Starvation Amdist Plenty", *The Daily Star*, August 26, 2001. http://www.dailystarnews.com/law/200108/03/lawwatch.htm

United Nations. Economic and Social Council. Committee on Economic, Social and Cultural Rights. *Substantive Issues Arising in the Implementation of the International Covenant on Economic, Social and Cultural Rights: General Comment 12 (Twentieth Session, 1999) The Right to Adequate Food (art. 11)* (Geneva: ECOSOC E/C.12/1999/5). www.unhchr.ch/tbs/doc.nsf/MasterFrameView/3d02758c707031d58025677f003b73b9? Opendocument

United Nations Children's Fund, *The State of the World's Children* (New York: UNICEF, 2002). http://www.unicef.org/sowc02summary/table1.html

Universal Declaration of Human Rights. http://www.unhchr.ch/udhr/index.htm

Venkatesan, J., "Food Must Reach the Starving, Not Rot: S.C.", *The Hindu*, August 21, 2001. http://www.hinduonnet.com/thehindu/2001/08/21/stories/01210001.htm

Index

Academic institutions, 125
Accessibility, 96, 102, 132
Accountability, 163-64
Agriculture, 125-26, 153
  employment in, 133
All India Anna Dravida Munnetra Kazhagam (AIADMK), 47, 128, 143
Allocation of foodgrains, 30, 36
Alternative and Innovative Education (AIE) Centres, 25
Andhra Pradesh,
  dropout rates, 116-17
  enrolments of students, 116-17
  implementation of scheme, 75
  mid-day meal scheme, 67-67
  menu of, 68-69, 137-38
  results of students, 116-17
  State Level Steering-*cum*-Monitoring Committee, of, 69, 70-72
Andhra Pradesh Primary Education Project, 33
Annapurna scheme, 156
Antyodaya Anna Yojana, 156
Ashram schools, 15

Baptla Mandal, 131
Beneficiaries, 46-48, 105-07, 134-35
Bihar Education Project, 33
Block Development Officer (BDO), 140
Block Level Steering-*cum*-Monitoring Committee, 52, 66, 137
Block system, 42
BPL Pregnent Women, 156
Brotherhood atmosphere, 138-39

Central Assistance, 27-28
Centrally sponsored scheme, 21, 24, 28
Child labour, 35, 105, 132
Child marriage, 35
Child Welfare Centres, 128
Community, arrangement of lunch, 146
Community development blocks, 129
Convention on Rights of Child, 157-58
Convergence cost, 108
Cooked Mid-day meal programme, 53
Cooking cost, 25-27
Coordination between scheme and education, 31
Corporate agencies, 21

Desperate attitude, 133-34
Destitute children, 155

Development of Women and Children in Rural Areas (DWCRA), 17, 18
Discipline, 109, 138-39
District Institute of Educational Training (DIET), 33, 99, 104
District Level Steering-*cum*-Monitoring Committee, 51, 64, 71, 78
District Primary Education Programme (DPEP), 31
Donation, 54
Dravida Munnetra Kazhagam (DMK), 47, 128, 143
Drop-out rates, 35, 109-10, 116-17, 119-20, 125-26, 132-34

Economic constraints, 35, 109
Education, dimensions of, 15
  financial assistance for, 127
  importance of, 133
  modernization of, 15
Education Guarantee Scheme (EGS), 25, 82
Educational programmes, 18
Educational systems, 99-100
Eighth Five Year Plan, 32
Electricity, availability of, 96
Elementary education, 67-68, 100
  role of government for, 32-33
Employment, 138
  opportunities, 132
Employment Assurance Scheme, 156
Enrolments of students, 19-20, 34-35, 109-10, 112-15, 130-32
Enthusiasm, 132
Episodic events, 153
Essential commodities, 149
Expenditure, 107-08, 128-30, 135-36

Fair Price shops, 62, 134, 138
Famine Code, 154
Feeding programme, 19, 46
Feeding scale cost, 46, 54
Financial assistance, 134-36
  allotment of, 147
Flexibility, 132
Flow of Funds, 74, 80, 86, 147
Food assistance programme, 154
Food Corporation of India (FCI), 16, 21, 25, 27
Food for Work Programme, 156
Food security, 159
Foodgrains supply, 55-56, 61-62, 85-86, 134-35, 142, 148-50
  mechanism of, 73, 79-80
Free for Education programme, 53

George Kent, 153
Government of India, grant financial assistance, 15
Government programmes, 154
Gram Panchayat Level Committee, 129, 136-37
Gram Panchayat Steering-*cum*-Monitoring Committee, 140-41
Gram Sabha, 17
Grassroots level, implementation scheme of, 16-17, 143-44

Gross Domestic Product (GDP), 153
Gujarat, cooked mid-day meal programme, 53
drop-out rates of, 112-13
menu of, 137
enrolment of students, 112-13
foodgrains supply of, 55-56
mid-day meal scheme, implementation of, 56
Gujarat Bal Nidhi Fund, 57

Hill Transport Subsidy (HTS), 25
Himachal Pradesh,
drop-out of students, 114-15
enrolments of students, 114-15
feeding scale in tribal and non-tribal areas, 61
mid-day meal scheme of, 60-62
administrative set up for, 63-64
State Level Steering-*cum*-Monitoring Committee, 63
weakly menu of, 137
Hot cooked food, 61

Illiterate family, 35
Implementing Agency, 69-70
India's Right system, 162-63
Industrialization, 35, 137
Infectious diseases, 161
Infrastructural facilities, 95-96, 131, 142
Integrated Child Development Scheme (ICDS), 17, 156, 163
International Covenant on economic, 157
International Society for Krishna Consciousness (ISKCON), 68, 69, 138
Irla Mandal, 131

Jawahar Rojgar Yojana (JRY), 104, 138
Jhansi District, 131

Kalahasti Temple Trust, 68, 69, 138
Kamraj, K. (former Chief Minister of Tamil Nadu), 45
Kitchen sheds, 137-39
availability of, 98-99, 104
schemes in, 104

Lavatory availability, 97, 102
Local Level management, 29-30
Lok Jumbish and Shiksha Karmi Project, Rajasthan, 33

Madhyamik Shiksha Kendras, 82
Mahatma Gandhi National Rural Employment Guarantee Scheme (MGNREGS), 149
Malnutrition, 16-18
Management, Monitoring and Evaluation (MME), 28

Mandal Development Officer (MDO), 140
Mandal Level Streeing-*cum*-Monitoring Committee, 140
Mandal system, 42
Mechanisms, 131, 139
Menu, formation of, 21-22, 68-69, 137
Mid-day meal scheme, 15, 18, 36-40, 53-54, 127, 132, 156
  central assistance admissible to States/UTs, 151-52
  cooking cost and calorific value, 82-83
  components of, 20-21
  district-wise status of, 106-08
  effectiveness of, 17-19
  facilities of, 105-06
  impact of, 109-10
  implementation of, 23-25, 56, 132-33
  infrastructure of, 26-27
  menu for, 21-22, 68-69, 137
  objectives of, 26
  problems of, 105
  programme of, 18-19
  revision of, 26-28
Mid-day Meal Scheme Committee (MDMSC), 142, 143, 148
  report of, 18-19
Migration, 35, 105, 125, 132
Modernization, 127
Monitoring mechanism, 131
Mother-Teacher Association (MTA), 129, 140-41

Naandi Foundation, 69
Narasimha Rao, P.V. (former Prime Minister), 24
National Benefit Maternity Scheme, 156
National Old-Age Pension Scheme, 156
National Policy on Education (NPE), 32
National Programme of Nutrition Support to Primary Education, 15, 24, 26, 127
National Rural Employment Guarantee Scheme (NREGS), 43
Nehru Yuvak Kendras (NYKs), 29
Ninth Five Year Plan, 34
Nodal department, 28-29
Noon meals programmes, 45, 49
Non-Governmental Organizations (NGOs), 16, 17, 29, 54, 69, 70, 83
Nutrition assessment, 46
Nutrition Support to Primary Education (NSPE), national programme for, 67

Obligations, categories of, 159-60
Operation Black Board Scheme, 33

Panchayat fund, 104
Panchayat Level Committee, 72
Panchayat Level Steering-*cum*-Monitoring Committee, 53, 59, 66

Panchayat Samities, 17
Parent-Teacher Association, 17, 29, 129, 140-41
People's Union of Civil Liberties (PUCL), 154
Plan of Action, 158
Planning Commission, 23
Political parties, 126
Poverty, 35, 105, 109, 136
Pradhan Mantri Gramodaya Yojana (PMGY), 26
Primary education, universalization of, 15-18, 127-28
Primary school children, mid-day meal programmes of, 18-19
Principal Distribution Centres (PDCs), 25
Programme of Action (PoA), 32
Provision of Central Assistance, 25-26
Public Corporate, 22
Public Distribution System, 156
Puratchi Thaaivar MGR Nutrition Programme, 45

Quality of Education, 147-48
Quality of food, 52, 72

Ramachandran, M.G. (former Chief Minister of T.N.), 45, 128
Rama Rao, N.T. (former Chief Minister of A.P.), 44
Recommendations, 148-49
Reimbursement, 27
Remuneration, 136-40
Right of Child, 133
Right to food internationally, 156-57
Rooms in sample schools, 98, 103
Rural areas, 132

Sabarkanta district, District Level Steering-*cum*-Monitoring Committee, 57-58
Safe drinking water, 101, 142
  availability of, 96, 100
Sampurna Gramin Yajana, 156
Sarva Shiksha Abhiyan (SSA), 34, 82, 84, 104, 126, 135, 138, 141-42, 146
Scheduled Castes and Scheduled Tribes, 15, 127
  population and literacy rate of, 33-34
School premises, basic facilities of, 146-47
Self-employment, 149
Self-Help Groups (SHGs), 25, 29, 69-70, 129, 136, 141, 149
Semi-urban areas, 132
Seventh Five Year Plan, 19, 24
Sixth Five Year Plan, 18
Social and Cultural Rights, 157
Starvation, 160-61
State Level Steering-*cum*-Monitoring Committee, 48, 50-52, 58, 63, 70-72, 77, 137, 140-42
  functions of, 30-32, 50-52
  physical structure of, 63-64
Subsidized foods, 154

Supreme Court of India, 67, 133, 155-56
Sustainability, 159
Swarnajayanti Gram Rojgar Yojana (SGRY), 17, 43, 57, 99, 104, 137, 138

Taluk Development Officer (TDO), 140
Taluk Level Steering-*cum*-Monitoring Committee, 59
Tamil Nadu,
  drop-out rates in, 110-11
  enrolment of students, 110-11
  foodgrains supply of, 47-48
  menu of, 137-38
  mid-day meal scheme in, 45-46, 128-30
Targeted Public Distribution Scheme, 156
Transportation cost, 54, 134-35
Tribal areas, 42
Tribal-Sub-Plan, 57, 137
  funds of, 99
Types of food, 137

Unemployment, 136
United Nations International Children Emergency Fund (UNICEF), 57, 161
Universal Declaration of Human Rights, 157
Universalisation of Elementary Education (UEE), 17
Untied funds, 104
Urban areas, 29, 69-70
Urbanization, 35
Utilization Certificate, 74, 86, 137
Utilization of funds, responsibility of, 147
Uttar Pradesh,
  administrative set up for implementation scheme, 82
  Block Level Steering-*cum*-Monitoring Committee, 78
  cooked food in rural areas, 77
  District Level Steering-*cum*-Monitoring Committee, 78
  drop-out rates of, 119-20
  enrolment of students, 11-20
  Gram Panchayat Level Steering-*cum*-Monitoring Committee, 78
  menu of, 137-38
  mid-day meal scheme, 76-78
  quality of foodgrains, 72
  State Level Steering-*cum*-Monitoring Committee, 77
Uttar Pradesh Basic Education Project, 33

Vatigonda Mandal, 131
Vidhya Volunteers, 104, 142
Village Education Committee (VEC), 17, 25, 29, 31, 85, 126, 141-42, 143, 148
Visakhapatnam, 69

Voluntary Support by Community, 31-32

Wage employment, 149
West Bengal, administrative set up for implementation scheme, 87
- Block Level Steering-*cum*-Monitoring Committee, 85
- cooked food in rural areas, 83
- District Level Steering-*cum*-Monitoring Committee, 84
- enrolement of student, 122-24
- mid-day meal scheme in, 82-84
- State Level Steering-*cum*-Monitoring Committee, 84
- weekly menu of, 83, 137-38

World Bank, 45
World Health Organization (WHO), 57, 161

Youth Clubs, 29

Zilla Parishad, 17